THE
FARNBOROUGH
FLYER

Nº 4472

Symphony in Steam

Written and Photographed
by
COLIN D. GARRATT

With a Foreword
by
O. S. NOCK

LONDON
BLANDFORD PRESS
Printed In Great Britain

First Published in 1970

Copyright © 1970 Blandford Press Ltd,
167 High Holborn, London WCIV 6PH

ISBN 0 7137 0528 0

Colour section printed in 4 colour photogravure by D. H. Greaves
Ltd, Scarborough.
Text Computer Typeset in 9 pt Baskerville, printed and bound by
C. Tinling & Co. Ltd, London and Prescot

Contents

DEDICATION

To Ken Colyer . . . Jazz Trumpet Player and Bandleader

Foreword

In years to come historians and sociologists may well find it difficult to explain the extraordinary fascination exercised over so many by the steam locomotive. That it has long since passed far beyond the childish attraction of the simple 'puff-puff' is widely acknowledged, when its devotees range from the top-ranking industrialists, barristers, and high dignitaries of the Church to humble mechanics who delight in using their skill in making beautiful models of favourite engines. It is also understandable that engineers who have been trained and spent a lifetime in steam should take pleasure in recalling nostalgically the machines which they knew so well. All this can be attributed to the sentimentality that is in all of us, which treasures its memories and is apt to bore others with its reminiscences.

On the other hand how could one explain the equal fascination that the steam locomotive has come to exercise over a rising generation which cannot have known the British railways in the age of steam? The present age is one in which steam is officially discredited by those in the highest authority, and one in which the survivors of the great steam age are being scrapped as fast as the breaker's yard can cope with them. It is an age when the railways themselves are in many quarters regarded as a dying industry, and the attention of youth is drawn to 'Jumbo Jets', and other innovations of the 1970s.

Yet here, in this book, is the work of a young man so captivated by the spectacle of steam locomotives in action as to devote literary and artistic talents to a work that he has called 'Symphony in Steam'. And a symphony it undoubtedly is. Older railway enthusiasts could well comment that he is trying to make bricks without straw, and that shots of dirty, unkempt mixed-traffic engines, grisly scenes in the breakers' yards, sheds with the sunshine streaming through gaps in the roofs to reveal something of the dirt and squalor inside do not contribute to a symphony. But that is to miss the point. It is that the irresistible fascination of the steam locomotive has fired a young man to find poetry and music in this dying scene, and to bring out his literary talents, his artistic instincts and his skill with a camera into the production of an arresting synthesis of the spirit that lies behind steam.

Colin Garratt's enthusiasm is as fresh and youthful as his own slender years; but into that brief period he has not only packed many a long photographic itinerary, but an immense amount of railway reading. He would probably be surprised to think he had written a 'period piece'; but that is what his 'Symphony in Steam' really is. Future generations of enthusiasts may not turn to his illustrations for historical details of locomotives because these are much more elaborately and comprehensively covered elsewhere; but his pictures record in superb detail the death of steam on the railways of Britain, and whether one sees it as cynical or macabre it is a 'documentary' worth the closest study.

Brnock

Introduction

I didn't believe it! – Well if it was going to happen it would not be before we were all very old. But now thinking back, I can so clearly recall my father showing me the headlines of the national papers that morning in 1955 when they announced the Modernisation Plan.

For some years prior to that announcement steam railways had been part of my life. I remember before I was 10 the long and happy summer days at the lineside, the rushing out to the railway after school and just a few years later my first trip to a distant town to see new and 'rare' engines.

Steam engines were a part of the world! – an institution as permanent as the streets upon which we walked and they certainly would not disappear just because the Government had drawn up a plan. Governments were always drawing up plans and even if they did carry them through, it was bound to take ten times longer than they said. Everyone at the lineside agreed, so we didn't worry about it.

Such was the faith of adolescence, but before many years had passed our whole world had collapsed, the magic was scattered and the most awe-inspiring of man's creations disappeared from our homelands.

But why 'Symphony in Steam'? Simply that I have endeavoured to present in picture form these childhood impressions of locomotives in the hope of communicating some of the magic to you. Further to this, I have given in the various articles details of the wider environmental aspects of the steam locomotive and attempted to harmonise them with the art work.

I make no claim to having created an encyclopaedic history of railways or to have included every possible type of locomotive. I have simply striven to give a feeling of adventure and to encourage the reader into further interest.

A love for locomotives is undoubtedly an emotional affair but the social, historical, geographical and technical aspects of the subject border so closely that some of these needed to be included. In short, then, I have endeavoured to combine the romance of steam along with some aspects of its historical connotation.

The symphonic title was chosen because of the showing of different facets and moods of the steam locomotive and these have been arranged into six sections called movements, thus drawing an analogy with musical symphonic construction.

The art work has been created after many wonderful adventures which have necessitated thousands of miles of travel in addition to the many hours spent waiting at the trackside. Of all the efforts involved, the greatest was the transference of one's feelings on to film. It was this effort that made the filming so exciting, for one was capturing a living thing, and it was the essence of this life – the essence of a moment in time – that I strove to capture.

I shall never forget the incursions into 'steam territories', the sight of the first steam engine, the sweet sooty smell of the depots and the skilful convincing of railway officials that we were worthy enough to remain on the 'right side of the fence' without a permit!

We always had a campaign to find bed and breakfast houses that overlooked the railway and so typical of our experiences was the Lancashire landlady who upon learning of our business in the town incredulously pronounced 'Wat the cum arlt wey up from Midlands tut see yon lawcaws!'

Other happy memories were relaxing over late night meals after a full day's filming, though perhaps not so pleasant was the subsequent pleading with landladies for an early (dawn) breakfast in order that we might be away by daybreak – after all it was not every day that one could see steam engines!

Perhaps one of the loveliest memories of all was one September night in 1967 whilst we were spending four days filming on Shap Bank, Westmorland. We were staying at a farmhouse set amongst the fells which overlooked the railway. Everyone had retired and at 1.00 a.m. the cry of a Britannia's whistle rang out across the lonely fells as the engine prepared to start the long climb up from Tebay.

The barking exhaust cut through the stillness as it resounded over the hills and the heavy Pacific forged its way up the bank with a northbound freight. From my bedroom window I watched it approach with blazing coals being flung out of the chimney and the cab bathed in a flickering orange glow that reflected in the smoke trail. Spellbound, I watched the drama and listened to the rhythms – for surely a living presence was passing through the fells that night.

But I must recount no more and proceed to give an account of when the various pictures were taken. The Southern Region work constitutes the oldest set and was done principally in the Bournemouth area during 1966/67 whilst the remainder of the British Railways work was completed in the north of England in 1967/68. The majority of the French pictures came from a lineside base in 1968 and the German ones were the result of an extensive tour of that country in the summer of 1969.

On the industrial side, the coalfields were filmed in 1967 and the Storefield and Stewarts and Lloyds Ironstone in the fall of 1968. The last to be made were the Cranford and Nassington pictures which were completed towards the end of 1969.

Like many other great things, steam locomotives have a capacity to give people pleasure and this is my reason for producing this volume. If the artwork is a retention of childhood impressions then it is all the richer for that and if the text awakens further interest then that too is the richer for it.

The book's background has been an enjoyable one and it is now doubly pleasant because I am able to share it with you.

In conclusion I wish to thank the following friends for their willing help . . . J. A. Morrison, Stoker Redfearn, F. Berry, Rev. Teddy Boston, Dr D. McNeil, Professor J. Simmons, D. Thornhill, T. D. A. Civil and K. P. Plant, Rowley James, Eric Tonks, John F. Clay and also Naylor Benzon Ltd. In addition to the above my very good friends Bill Parkes and Horace Gamble have both made valuable suggestions and many happy evenings were spent with them in checking details and m/s.

If this be insufficient then my greatest thanks of all is to Judy Warner for her encouragement and typing of the m/s and also to O. S. Nock for preparing a 'celebrity's' introduction.

March 1970   Colin D. Garratt

Linkage Chart

This is designed to provide a cross-reference between the descriptive pages and the colour plates.

1st Movement

PRELUDE

Locomotives on Shed

1 **Preserved engines at Tyseley** (1). Ex-G.W.R. design Castle Class 4–6–0 *Clun Castle*.

2 **Sunshine smoke and shadow.** Two ex-Est 141TB tank engines in the roundhouse at Nogent Vincennes.

3 **Shades of pastel.** A vintage Etat 140C simmers gently on the turntable at Verdun.

4 **Tanks—Nord style.** A 141TC and an 040TG at Joncherolles.

5 **Front ends.** Two ex-L.M.S. 5MT 4–6–0s at Crewe (South).

6 **Rays at Rose Grove (1)**. Ex-L.M.S. 8F 2–8–0s.

7 **Rays at Rose Grove (2)**. An ex-L.M.S. 5MT 4–6–0 and ex-L.M.S. 8F 2–8–0s.

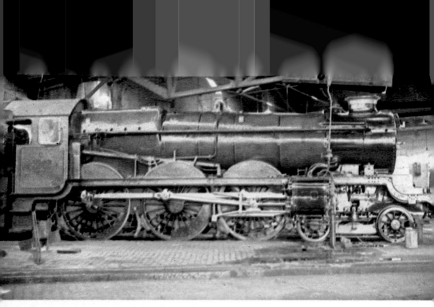

8 **Preserved engines at Tyseley** (2). Ex-G.W.R. design Castle Class 4–6–0 *Clun Castle*—note the double chimney.

9 **Preserved engines at Tyseley** (3). Ex-G.W.R. Class 1600 0–6–0 Pannier Tank.

10 **Castle at Chester.** Ex-G.W.R. Castle Class 4–6–0 *Pendennis Castle* arrives on shed after working an enthusiasts' special.

11 **Restoration at Leicester.** An ex-G.C.R. 2–8–0 a

ex-L.N.E.R. V2 2–6–2, *Green Arrow*, being restored.

12 **Studies in valve gear** (1). The Walschaerts valve gear of a B.R. Standard 4MT 4–6–0.

13 **Studies in valve gear** (2). The Walschaerts valve gear of a D.B. Class 044 2–10–0.

14 **Lighting up.** Two ex-L.M.S. 5MT 4–6–0s and an ex-L.M.S. 8F 2–8–0 at Lostock Hall having just been lit up on a Sunday afternoon in readiness for the new week's workings.

15 **Burnished gold.** A.D.B. Class 044 2–10–0 at Paderborn.

16 **Oil and steam.** Ex-L.M.S. 5MT 4–6–0s at Blackpool.

17 **Smoke vents.** Ex-L.M.S. 8F 2–8–0s at Rose Grove.

18 **Study in chimneys.** Chimney of an ex-L.M.S. 5MT 4–6–0.

19 **On the ash pits.** An ex-L.M.S. 8F 2–8–0 has its smokebox cleaned out before entering the depot at Croes Newydd.

20 **The Fitter.** Last-minute attentions ex-L.M.S. 8F 2–8–0s at Rose Grov

21 **Engines and Men.** Ex-L.M.S. 8F 2–8–0s at Northwich.

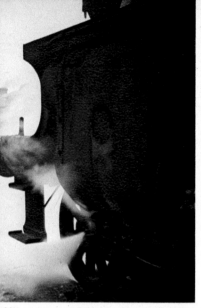

Silhouettes and steam. Two ex-L.M.S. 5MT 4–6–0s at Newton Heath.

23 **Ready for the road.** An ex-L.M.S. 5MT 4–6–0 rumbles out of the depot at Newton Heath.

24 **Standards at Bournemouth.** B.R. Standard 4MT 4–6–0 and 5MT 4–6–0 await their next turn of duty.

25 **Smokey magic.** A D.B. Class 052 2–10–0 at Saarbrücken.

26 **Giants at Rheine.** A D.B. Class 012 4–6–2 and Class 042 2–8–2 in the depot yards.

27 **The big three.** A D.B. Class 050 and two Class 052 2–10–0s at Limburg depot.

28 **With steam to spare.** A B.R. Standard 9F at Crewe (South).

29 **Standby engine.** An ex-L.M.S. 8F 2–8–0 on standby duty at Crewe (South).

30 **Bournemouth miscellany.** Line up of power at Bournemouth depot. L–R: ex-L.M.S. 2–6–2T, B.R. Standard 4MT 2–6–0, B.R. Standard 5MT 4–6–0, B.R. Standard 4MT 2–6–0, B.R. Standard 4MT 2–6–4 Tank.

31 **Paris suburban.** Ex-Nord 141TC tank engines used for working suburban traffic from Gare du Nord in Paris at their depot at Joncherolles.

2nd Movement

SCHERZO

Locomotives at Work

32 **Summer in the New Forest.** Rebuilt ex-S.R. West Country Class 4–6–2 *Axminster* approaching Brockenhurst with a Waterloo–Bournemouth express.

33 In full cry. A D.B. Class 043 2–10–0 at work near Meppen.

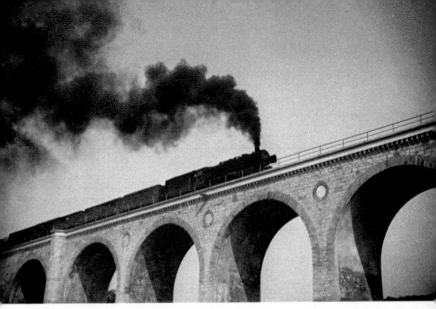

34 Viaduct studies (1). A D.B. Class 044 2–10–0 heads an east-bound freight between Paderborn and Altenbeken.

35 Viaduct studies (2). A D.B. Class 044 2–10–0 heads an east-bound freight between Paderborn and Altenbeken.

36 **Golden Arrow.** The south-bound *Flèche d'Or* headed by an e

L.M. 231G passes a lineside apple orchard south of Rang du Fliers.

37 **Shrouded in smoke and steam.** A B.R. Standard 5MT 4–6–0 climbs out of Weymouth with a London-bound express.

38 **Last steam train from Weymouth.** A B.R. Standard 5MT climbs Upwey Bank with a fruit special from Weymouth Docks.

39 **Against the wind.** Rebuilt ex-S.R. Merchant Navy Class 4–6–2 *Orient Line* speeds across the water at Poole with an up local train.

40 **With rhythmic stealth.** Rebuilt ex-S.R. West Country Class 4–6–2 *Honiton* leaves Bournemouth with an express for Weymouth.

41 **Sylvan setting.** A D.B. Class 044 2–10–0 with a north-bound freight train near Lingen.

42 **Raising the echoes.** A D.B. Class 044 2–10–0 fills the woodlands with sound as it storms the climb southwards from Bullay.

43 **Into the depths.** After climbing up from Bullay a D.B. Class 044 2–10–0 dives into the tunnel at Kinderbeurner.

44 **. . . And out again.** A D.B. Class 044 2–10–0 breaks into the open again after passing through Bullay tunnel.

45　**Outlines in black and gold.** With Altenbeken to the rear a D.B. Class 044 2–10–0 heads for the tunnel with a heavy freight.

46 **Easter special.** S.N.C.F. American-built 141R races for Amiens with an Easter holiday extra.

47 **With rapid acceleration.** S.N.C.F. American-built 141R heads a south-bound stopping train away from Rang du Fliers.

48 **Drama in the meadows.** An ex-P.L.M. 231G and an American-built 141R speed through the countryside near Rue with an express for Paris.

49 **Morning glory.** A D.B. Class 044 2–10–0 contrasts with the sunrise in the Mosel Valley.

50 **Pacific power.** A D.B. Class 012 4–6–2 pauses briefly at Lingen with a north-bound express.

51 **Hoppers for the Saar.** A D.B. Class 044 2–10–0 crosses the river Mosel at Bullay.

52 **The beauty of Arnside** (1). An east-bound freight passing through the station, headed by an ex-L.M.S. 5MT 4–6–0.

53 **The beauty of Arnside (2).** A B.R. Standard 4MT 4–6–0 crosses the viaduct with a freight from Ulverston.

54 **The waters of the Lune.** Ex-L.M.S. 5MT 4–6–0 crosses Melling viaduct and heads for Carnforth with a trip freight.

55 **Preserved glory (1).** Ex-G.W.R. 4500 Class 2–6–2 Tank at Buckfastleigh on the privately owned Dart Valley Railway.

56 **Preserved glory (2).** Ex-G.W.R. 1400 Class 0–4–2 Tank at Buckfastleigh on the Dart Valley Railway.

57 **Preserved glory (3).** Ex-L.N.E.R. A4 4–6–2 *Sir Nigel Gresley* at Bournemouth.

58 **High summer.** A B.R. Standard 5MT 4–6–0 leaves Bournemouth with a train for Weymouth.

59 **Patterns and colour.** A south-bound exp

r Meppen headed by D.B. Class 042 2–8–2.

60 **Commemorative specials (1).** Two ex-L.M.S. 5MT 4–6–0s on the climb to Copey Pit summit with an enthusiasts' special which formed a part of the commemorations to mark the ending of steam power on British Rail.

51 Stranger on the Southern. Ex-L.N.E.R. A4 4–6–2 *Sir Nigel Gresley* brings the coaching stock up to Bournemouth Central for the return working of an enthusiasts' special to Waterloo.

52 Commemorative specials (2). Two B.R. Standard 4MT 4–6–0s with another enthusiasts' special marking the end of steam power on British Rail, seen here approaching Skipton.

63 **Bound for the capital.** Rebuilt ex-S.R. West Country Class 4–6–2 *Dartmoor* arrives at Bournemouth Central with an express for Waterloo.

64 **Through the pine cuttings.** Rebuilt ex-S.R. West Country Class 4–6–2 *Dartmoor* speeds away from Bournemouth with a train for Weymouth.

65 **Station pilot.** A B.R. Standard 3MT 2–6–0 near Parkstone having worked an empty stock train out of Bournemouth Central.

66   French grandiose. An ex-P.L.M. 231G speeds a Calais–Paris express southwards near Rue.

67 **Deep in the forest.** Unrebuilt ex-S.R. West Country Class 4–6–2 *Bude* passes through the New Forest with an express for Waterloo.

68 **Encroaching modernisation.** An ex-L.M.S. Jinty Class 3F 0–6–0 and a B.R. Standard 2MT 2–6–0 on shunting duties at Crewe.

69 **Eruption.** An ex-L.M.S. 5MT 4–6–0 approaches the tunnel at Melling with a morning pick-up freight.

70 **With speed in the 70s.** A D.B. Class 012 4–6–2 pounds over the river Ems with a south-bound express.

71 **Through Dorset pastures.** A B.R. Standard 4MT 2–6–0 with a local train west of Wareham.

72 Pines and Pullmans. Rebuilt ex-S.R. West Country Class 4–6–2 *Oakhampton* passes Lyndhurst Road with the west-bound *Bournemouth Belle*.

73 Shades of evening. Rebuilt ex-S.R. Merchant Navy Class 4–6–2 *Elder Dempster Lines* with a Weymouth–Bournemouth local train.

74 **With a cry from the whistle.** A D.B. Class 044 2–10–0 prepares to enter Kinderbeurner tunnel with a heavy south-bound freight train.

75 **Power personified.** An early morning mixed freight headed by a D.B. Class 044
2–10–0 heads south along the Mosel Valley route.

76 **Lineside rhododendrons.** A B.R. Standard 5MT 4–6–0 with a Waterloo–Weymouth express approaching Poole.

77 **With a flurry of smoke.** Rebuilt ex-S.R. Merchant Navy Class 4–6–2 *United States Lines* dashes down Parkstone Bank with an express for Weymouth.

78 **South-bound stopper.** A D.B. Class 023 2–6–2 leaves the tunnel at Bullay with a passenger train for Saarbrücken.

3rd Movement

NOCTURNE

Locomotives at Night

79 **Sunset at the viaduct.** A D.B. Class 044 2–10–0 heads eastwards between Paderborn and Altenbeken.

80 **Dusk at Bullay.** A hopper train headed by tw

8. Class 044 2-10-0s tackles the gradient out of Bullay.

81 **Midnight at Carnforth** (1). B.R. Standard 4MT 4–6–0 confronts B.R. Standard Britannia Class 4–6–2 *Oliver Cromwell*.

Midnight at Carnforth (2). B.R.
Standard 4MT 4–6–0 and Ex-
L.M.S. 8F 2–8–0.

83 Midnight at Carnforth (3). B.R.
Standard 4MT 4–6–0.

4 Midnight at Carnforth (4). Ex-
L.M.S. 5MT 4–6–0.

85 Midnight at Carlisle Kingmoor.
B.R. Standard Britannia Class 4–6–2
Lord Rowallan.

86 **Breathless for dawn.** An ex-L.M.S. 8F 2–8–0 in readiness for duty at Carnforth.

87 **Sunstreak.** The setting sun catches the side of a Waterloo-bound express in the New Forest headed by a B.R. Standard 5MT 4-6-0.

8 **The final hour.** B.R. Standard Britannia Class 4-6-2 *Oliver Cromwell* leaves Lostock Hall depot.

89 **Points.** Track and sunset at Lostock Hall.

90 **Study in outline.** Silhouette of
ex-L.M.S. 8F 2–8–0 and a B.
Standard 4MT 4–6–0 under the a
lamps at Carnforth.

91 **Early hours in the freight yards (1).** An ex-L.M.S. 8F 2–8–0 assembles a night
freight train in Carnforth Yards.

92 **Early hours in the freight yards (2).** An ex-L.M.S. 8F 2–8–0 pulls heavily out of Carnforth Yards with a freight for Burnley.

93 **Night action.** An ex-L.M.S. 8F disturbs the silence as it thunders a night-time freight southwards from Carnforth.

94 Sun, water and silhouette. A D.B. Class 044 2–10–0 crosses the river Mosel at Bullay.

95 **Dawn in the Mosel Valley.** An early freight train bound for Trier headed by a D.B. Class 044 2–10–0.

96 **Sunset over the Ems.** A north-bound coal train crosses the river Ems on the Rheine–Emden route with a D.B. Class 044 2–10–0 in charge.

97　**Silent sentinel.** A D.B. signal in the stop position.

98 **Thunder on the viaduct.** A D.B. Class 044 2–10–0 struggles with the climb towards Altenbeken with a Kassel-bound freight train.

99 **As the sun sets.** A D.B. Class 044 2–10–0 heads for Emden with a freight from Rheine.

100 **Morning splendour.** A D.B. Class 044 2–10–0 catches the early morning sun as it heads south along the Mosel Valley route.

4th Movement

EPISODE

Locomotives in Industry

101 **Autumn at Cranford.** A Hudswell Clark 0–6–0ST at Cranford Ironstone Quarry near Kettering.

102 **0–6–2 survivors** **(1)**. Robert Stephenson 0–6–2 Tank engine at Philadelphia Colliery.

103 **0–6–2 survivors** (2). A Kitson 0–6–2 Tank engine passes Shiney Row on the Philadelphia Colliery system.

104 **In the works (1).** Two Robert Stephenson and Hawthorn 0–6–0STs undergoing overhaul at Ashington Works.

105 **In the works (2).** A Robert Stephenson and Hawthorn 0–6–0 Tank engine undergoing overhaul at Ashington.

106 **In dockland.** A Bagnall 0–6–0ST *Enterp*

forms shunting operations at Preston Docks.

107 **Two's company.** NCB No. 49 a Robert Stephenson and Hawthorn 0–6–0ST with Giesl ejector and NCB No. 6 a Bagnall 0–6–0ST standing in the shed yard at Backworth Colliery.

108 **Sunlight and shadow.** NCB No. 33 a Hawthorn Leslie 0–4–0ST and NCB No. 11 a Hudswell Clarke 0–4–0ST at Philadelphia Colliery.

109 **Smoke screen.** A Hunslet 0–6–0ST fitted with a Giesl ejector at work on the Ashington Colliery system.

110 **A Great Western memory.** An ex-G.W.R. 1500 Class Tank engine finds a new lease of life at Coventry Colliery after being purchased by the National Coal Board.

111 **Early duty.** A Robert Stephenson and Hawthorn 0–6–0ST leaves the Pen Green depot of Stewarts & Lloyds at Corby before the break of dawn.

112 **Dawn at Stewarts & Lloyds (1).** Robert Stephenson and Hawthorn 0–6–0ST and the steelworks.

113 **Dawn at Stewarts & Lloyds (2).** Scene from the cab of a Kitson 0–6–0ST as it approaches the steelworks with an early-morning train.

114 **Duty commences at Cranford.** An Avonside 0–6–0ST framed by the shed entrance at Cranford Ironstone Quarry near Kettering.

115 **Under the arches.** A Robert Stephenson and Hawthorn 0–6–0ST on the Oakley Ironstone branch of the Stewarts & Lloyds' system with a special platelayers' train.

116 **Power at Pen Green.** L–R: A Robert Stephenson and Hawthorn 0–6–0ST, a Manning Wardle 0–6–0ST and two Kitson 0–6–0STs at the Pen Green depot of Stewarts & Lloyds, Corby.

117 **Engine with waggon.** One of the Stewarts & Lloyds (Steel Division) Hawthorn Leslie 0–6–0STs in yellow livery.

118 **Steam up.** L–R: Kitson 0–6–0ST *Caerphilly* and Andrew Barclay 0–4–0ST at Storefield Quarry near Corby.

119 **Activity.** Another view of the Kitson and Andrew Barclay locos at Storefield.

120 **Waiting for the road.** An Andrew Barclay 0–4–0ST stands at Storefield Quarry summit with a loaded train.

121 **Reflections on a theme.** Hunslet 0–6–0ST *Ring Haw* heads towards the quarry face at Nassington Ironstone Quarry.

122 **Panned action.** Hunslet 0–6–0ST *Ring Haw* at Nassington.

3 **Wayside berries.** Hunslet 0–6–0 ST *Jacks Green* brings a loaded train along the now defunct route between Peterborough and Rugby.

124 **Sunspot.** Hunslet 0–6–0ST *Jacks Green* at Nassington.

125 **Contrasts in colour.** An Andrew Barclay 0–6–0ST pulls away from the quarry face at Storefield.

126 **The long drag.** Hunslet 0–6–0S *Jacks Green* struggles up the ste͏ incline out of Nassington Quarr͏

127 **Rural retreat.** Hunslet 0–6–0ST *Jacks Green* assembles a train together at Nassington.

128 **Duty done.** A Bagnall 0–6–0͏ reaches the end of its day's w͏ at Cranford Ironstone Quarry.

5th Movement
FUNERAL MARCH
Locomotives in Decline

129 **Dereliction at Patricroft.** A B.R. Standard 5MT 4–6–0 and ex-L.M.S. 8F 2–8–0s
await their fate in the closed depot.

130   **Decay at Le Mans.** An ex-Etat 040TA is seen from the cab of an S.N.C.F. 141P
on the scrap line at Le Mans depot.

131 **Silence at Heaton Mersey.** Ex-L.M.S. 5MT 4–6–0 and 8F 2–8–0s linger on in their now-derelict depot.

132 **The end at Trafford Park.** An ex-L.M.S. 4MT 2–6–4T and 8F 2–8–0s await despatch to breakers' yards.

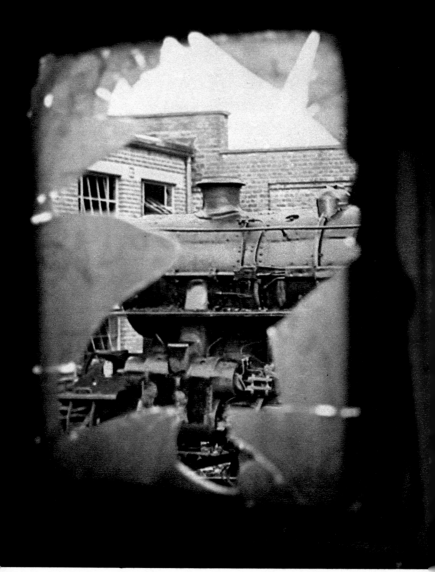

133 **Destruction.** Ex-L.M.S. design

...5–0 on the scrap line at Lostock Hall.

134 **Rust and burnt umber.** An ex-L.M.S. 5MT 4–6–0 awaits breaking-up at Kettering.

135 **The last B1.** An ex-L.N.E.R. B1
4–6–0 lies derelict at Low Moor.

136 **Mottles (1).** The broken roof of
Patricroft depot throws mottling
effects over an ex-L.M.S. 8F 2–8–0.

137 **Mottles (2).** Further mottling effects at Patricroft featuring ex-L.M.S. 8F 2–8–0s.

138 **Rust and grime.** Ex-W.D. Austerity 2–8–0 stands in the abandoned depot at Sunderland.

139 **Farewell to Carlisle Upperby.** Where the last engine to remain was a B.R. Standard 4MT 4–6–0.

6th Movement

FINALE

Locomotives in Scrapyards

140 **Cutting up.** Ex-L.M.S. 5MT 4–6–0 at Cohens' Yard, Kettering.

141 **Cutter's torch.** Smokebox cutting on an ex-L.M.S. 5MT 4–6–0, Cohens' Yard, Kettering.

142 **Executioner.** Smokebox cutti on an ex-L.M.S. 5MT 4–6– Cohens' Yard, Kettering.

143 **Reduction.** The frames and boiler tubes of an ex-L.M.S. 5MT 4–6–0 at Cohens' Yard, Kettering.

144 Breaker's yard. A scene at Cohens, Kettering, with driving axle and two ex-L.M.S. 5MT 4–6–0s.

145 **Acetylene blaze.** Bogie wheel cutting at Cohens, Kettering.

146 **Jig-saw in iron and steel.** Wheel remains at Cohens, Kettering.

147 **Tragic remains.** An ex-L.M. chimney lies on the ground Cohens' Yard, Kettering.

Descriptions to the Coloured Illustrations

Ex-L.N.E.R. A3 Flying Scotsman   Front endpaper
When railway historians see *Flying Scotsman* today, their minds must inevitably go back to the British Empire Exhibition at Wembley in 1924, when the locomotive, as an A1, stood alongside the G.W.R.'s *Caerphilly Castle*. Both were the latest achievements in British locomotive engineering. The G.W. authorities had proudly displayed a board on their engine stating it to be Britain's most powerful express passenger locomotive. This was challenged by the L.N.E.R. which led to the historic exchange test of 1925. The result of this exchange – which excited vast public interest – was a victory for the G.W.R. and led to Gresley modifying his A1 Pacifics with long travel valves and a boiler pressure increased from 180 lb per sq in. to 220 lb per sq in. The modified engines were reclassified A3.

Eventually this distinguished class totalled 79 engines of which *Flying Scotsman* remains the sole survivor. They had one of the best ranges of names in locomotive history, the majority commemorating famous racehorses.

On 14 January 1963 as B.R. No. 60103 it ended its public career after working from Kings Cross to Doncaster, where it had been built 40 years earlier. During those years it had covered over 2 million miles. Its long history contains many fascinating stories, perhaps the most famous of which was its operation of the inaugural run of the non-stop London to Edinburgh *Flying Scotsman* service on 1 May 1928. To facilitate this the engine – as were some of its sisters – was equipped with a corridor tender to enable change of engine crew *en route*. In 1934 it further distinguished itself by running from Kings Cross to Leeds in 2½ hours.

After withdrawal from service the locomotive was purchased by Mr. Alan Pegler and was restored to typical L.N.E.R. A3 appearance (she had been converted from an A1 in 1947). This purchase caused widespread attention and has over recent years aroused as much public interest as the modernisation programme of British Rail.

On 20 April 1963 she worked the Festiniog Railway's annual special from London as far as Ruabon and this was to be the first of numerous subsequent specials worked by *Flying Scotsman*. On that first run in preserved form no less than 8.000 people awaited her arrival at

Birmingham Snow Hill Station. Officially speaking the locomotive is based at Doncaster and Mr. Pegler commissioned the great L.N.E.R. driver Edgar Hoyle to help keep her in trim.

During the course of the engine's special journeys over B.R. there arose the problem of watering facilities and to overcome this a second tender has been fitted to ensure an adequate reserve.

On 1 May 1968 a 40th Anniversary non-stop run was successfully accomplished from Kings Cross to Edinburgh with a 330 ton train in $7\frac{3}{4}$ hours. The occasion was filmed throughout in colour by the B.B.C. and subsequently screened on television. Three days later the return trip was undertaken with the same loading and although speed was nowhere in excess of 80 m.p.h. the journey of 393 miles was covered in just over $7\frac{1}{2}$ hours. For a locomotive over 45 years old this was no mean feat and reflects even greater glory on the designer Sir Nigel Gresley who in the minds of many is remembered mainly for the all conquering streamlined A4s. Notwithstanding the unofficial 102 m.p.h. of the G.W.R. *City of Truro* it remains an historically authenticated fact that *Flying Scotsman* was the first British steam locomotive to pass the 100 m.p.h. mark, accurately timed by competent personnel and equipment. The plate shows the engine passing Newton Harcourt, near Leicester, with a south bound special.

Ex-G.W.R. Castle Class 4–6–0

Pl. 1, 8, 11

One could say many amazing things about these locomotives – a fact that is borne out by the perpetuation of the design virtually unchanged for almost 30 years. The first examples appeared in 1923 as direct descendents of Churchward's Star Class and by 1950 when the last series was built the class totalled 171 engines. Those built under nationalisation were improved to an even greater standard of performance by the fitting of higher degree superheat and some were given double chimneys. The only other change made was to the lubrication mechanism.

It is tempting to say that they were everyone's favourite, for apart from their devastating performances they were one of the finest looking locomotives ever to run in Great Britain. The vast majority of the class were named after castles but a few were dedicated to early G.W.R. personalities and fighter aircraft. The last one No. 7037, was named *Swindon* in memory of its being the last G.W. express passenger engine to be built at the famous Works.

For over 40 years they worked the top G.W. expresses from Paddington to Bristol, Exeter, Plymouth, Cardiff, Birmingham, Wolverhampton and Chester. Their history, being full of achievements, cannot be satisfactorily itemised here but $56\frac{1}{2}$ mins. for the 77 miles from Paddington to Swindon was one of their exploits. Apart from the several 100 m.p.h. bursts that have been recorded with them, their capacity for haulage was remarkable. In 1925 No. 4074 *Caldicot Castle* took the Cornish Riviera express loaded to 530 tons from Paddington to Westbury in 94 minutes for the 96 miles.

The class had 4 cylinders 16″ × 26″, a boiler pressure of 225 lb per sq in., and driving wheels of 6′ $8\frac{1}{2}$″ diameter.

Withdrawal commenced in 1959 and owing to the rapid dieselisation of the Western Region, the Castles had all gone by the mid-1960s. Originally three were preserved and reference is made to these on page 160. However, in 1970 came the news that a fourth example had been saved by the Great Western Railway Society. This was one of several of the type that have lain for some years in Woodham's Scrapyard at Barry.

Ex-Est 141TB Pl. 2

The 141TBs were originally a series of 112 engines of Class 11S built for the Est Railway between 1910 and 1917 for main line and suburban passenger work.

Their principal dimensions were 2 cylinders of $21\frac{1}{2}'' \times 26''$, boiler pressure 227 lb per sq in. and driving wheels 5' 2" diameter. Weight was 87 tons and length 45'. Officially speaking their maximum speed was 56 m.p.h. although they were easily capable of exceeding this figure.

They were found throughout Est territory, especially at the Gare de l'Est in Paris, and some of them were fitted for push and pull operation. They eventually replaced the Est 131TB Class of 1925.

Suburban passenger engines are especially vulnerable under modernisation schemes and during the 1960s withdrawal commenced. The last examples to remain in traffic were based at Nogent Vincennes depot in Paris, from which they operated the suburban trains out of Paris Bastille Station.

During recent years the 141TBs along with the larger 141TCs attracted many enthusiasts to Paris because these engines provided an historical link with pre-nationalisation designs and afforded a change from the American built 141Rs that are responsible for the vast majority of steam workings in the S.N.C.F.

Unfortunately the end came suddenly for the 141TB when in 1969 they were completely replaced by electrification and the remaining survivors withdrawn *en bloc*.

Ex-Etat 140C Pl. 3

This class comprised 370 engines that were built to an Etat design of 1913 for heavy freight working. During the first world war many were built to the order of the French Government and they became the French equivalent of Britain's 2-8-0 R.O.D. locomotives of the Great Central design. Some of the 140Cs were actually built in Britain by the North British Locomotive Co. of Glasgow. Building of the class continued up to 1920. During world war I they were prevalent throughout much of France and have remained widely spread in the country ever since.

They have 2 cylinders of $23'' \times 25\frac{1}{4}''$, a boiler pressure of 170 lb per sq in. and driving wheels of 4' $8\frac{1}{2}''$ diameter. A certain number of the class were fitted with either A.C.F.I. or Dabeg feedwater heaters, the presence of which was revealed by the two cylinders situated between the chimney and dome.

In common with their British R.O.D. counterparts they have had a long life and examples still remain in S.N.C.F. stock on the Ouest and Est regions. Those on the Est region are centred around Verdun which was the scene of much bitter fighting in both the world wars. Peace has now returned to Verdun and today it is one of the quietest and prettiest of

French towns, yet it seems appropriate that the area should still echo to the sounds of these old wartime veterans.

The Verdun engines work stone trains between Dungy and Conflans and many British enthusiasts have made the pilgrimage across France to see them in action. The survivors are maintained in a magnificent condition and have always seemed to me to be, visually speaking, a cross between the Jones Goods 4–6–0s of the Highland Railway and the G2 0–8–0s of the London and North Western.

Ex-Nord 0–4–0TG   Pl. 4

One of the Nord's standard shunting tanks, 80 locomotives being constructed between 1930–1933. They were a 20″ × 26″ 2-cylinder simple design with a boiler pressure of 170 lbs per sq in. and driving wheels of 4′ 2″ diameter.

An unusual feature of the design is the incorporation of outside Stephenson Link Motion, an arrangement frequently found on old, small French engines.

For many years the class was employed at principal depots throughout the Nord system but after a gradual demise the locomotive featured in our picture remains as the last survivor.

Ex-Nord 141TC   Pl. 4, 31

Undoubtedly the 141TCs are one of the most handsome and well proportioned tank engines still remaining in service. These impressive machines comprised a batch of 72 locomotives built between 1931 and 1935 to a design by de Caso. They were constructed for working the Paris suburban routes of the Nord system and are typically Nord in appearance. The class is fitted with boilers similar to those of the old 231C Nord Super Pacifics.

The design is a 25″ × 27½″ 2-cylinder superheated simple with a boiler pressure of 256 lbs per sq in. and driving wheels of 5′ 1″ diameter. By British standards such dimensions for a tank engine are considerable. The 141TCs weigh 121 tons and are 50′ long. The adequacy of these proportions is demonstrated by their ability to haul trains of 500 tons over gradients up to 1 in 200 at speeds of 70 m.p.h. Furthermore they can develop 2,000 indicated horse power.

Other interesting points are the Willison type automatic coupling, which is immensely useful in suburban work; and the Aubert control gear for push and pull working. Their valve gear is unusual, being of Cossart type which operates poppet valves.

Many are still at work in the Paris area allocated to Les Joncherolles and Beaumont depots for working suburban trains out of Gare du Nord.

Such good things are not to remain for long however, as work on the electrification of the suburban system is well under way and upon completion of this another of the distinctive French designs will pass into history.

Ex-L.M.S. 5MT 4–6–0   Pl. 5, 7, 14, 16, 18, 22–3,
                                                    52, 54, 60, 69, 84, 133–4

These, the famous 'Black 5s', were Britain's most successful general purpose locomotives. First introduced in 1934 by Stanier they have since become regarded as his masterpiece and no less than 842 were built, the final ones being well into B.R. days in 1951. They were ideal machines for a vast system like the L.M.S. and could be found between such extremes as the Wick – Bournemouth and Swansea – York routes. The Black 5s covered a multiplicity of duties ranging from express passenger work to the haulage of coal trains.

During the wartime effort they proved to be invaluable and consequently many were built privately by the Vulcan Foundry and Armstrong Whitworth. The leading details of the class were 2 cylinders of $18\frac{1}{2}'' \times 28''$, boiler pressure 225 lb per sq in., and a diameter of 6' for driving wheels. Their coal capacity was 9 tons and water capacity was 4,000 gallons.

Their emergence in such great numbers inevitably spelt the doom of older pre-grouping types especially those from the L.N.W.R. Such unfortunate circumstances however were partly offset by the pleasing features of the Black 5s, for they were most acceptable to everyone's mind. Four of the class were named. After the war a number of experimental modifications were made to them. A series was built with Caprotti valve gear instead of the traditional Walschaerts and one of the class was fitted with Stephenson Link Motion; this latter experiment was alleged to be extremely successful. Other modifications included some with roller bearings, a batch with steel fireboxes and a few with double chimneys.

It was long ago recognised that the Black 5 would be amongst the last British steam engines to remain in service and they continued to do excellent work right up to the final day. B.R.'s last steam train – the 15 gn. return special from Liverpool to Carlisle – was worked by two of them running in tandem and thus a fitting tribute was paid to so fine a class.

A grand total of 12 have been preserved and some of these are listed on page 161.

Ex-L.M.S. 8F 2-8-0

Pl. 6, 7, 14, 17, 19, 20–1, 29, 82, 86, 90–3, 129, 132–3, 136–7

British locomotive history is studded with innumerable designs and when one thinks back it is amazing to consider the incredible variety of engines that have come and gone in the last 150 years. Out of this array of thousands of locomotives it would be difficult to think of half a dozen types that ever exceeded a total of 700 engines. However, two such designs were produced in 1934/5 by William Stanier C.M.E. of the L.M.S. They were his 5MT 4-6-0s for mixed traffic duties and the 8F 2-8-0 heavy freight engines. The L.M.S. was a highly industrialised system and long before the outbreak of war the 8Fs had proved themselves to be invaluable.

In 1940 the type was adopted by the Ministry of Supply and orders were given for 300 locomotives. To meet this requirement some were built by Beyer Peacock of Manchester and the North British Locomotive Works at Glasgow, in addition to the Workshops of the L.N.E.R., G.W.R. and S.R.

Owing to the German advance in 1940 they were not needed on the Continent and many were loaned to the L.M.S. before being despatched to the Middle East in 1941/42 where they were used in the Western Desert. During these years they appeared in such places as Egypt, Palestine, Iraq and Persia, many never returning home. In fact 22 were later purchased by the Turkish State Railways and 40 by the Egyptian Railways. It is rumoured that some are still at work in the Middle East. Many, however, did return and the last ones were put into Midland Region stock as late as 1957.

The engines did well and their suitability for long distance freight haulage is born out by their adequate dimensions. They are a 2-cylinder type of $18\frac{1}{2}'' \times 28''$ proportions with a boiler pressure of 225 lbs per sq in., driving wheels of $4' 8\frac{1}{2}''$ diameter and a coal and water capacity of 9 tons and 4,000 gallons respectively.

After the war when the railways returned to normal operation, the majority of the class passed to the L.M.S. and became particularly widespread in the Midlands. Many were based at Toton and Wellingborough for the operation of coal and iron ore traffic. Sixty-eight were purchased by the L.N.E.R. but after nationalisation these became absorbed by the Midland region.

As our illustrations clearly show, they survived until the end of steam on B.R. and one of their very last duties was the midnight freight train from Carnforth to Burnley shown on plate nos. 91-3. Only one has been preserved which is now in the good care of the Severn Valley Railway at Bridgnorth; it is one of the wartime engines that did service in the Middle East. The locomotive is owned by the 8F Preservation Society.

Ex-G.W.R. 1600 Class 0–6–0PT

Pl. 9

After F. W. Hawksworth succeeded Charles Collett as C.M.E. of the G.W.R., he produced a lightweight design of Pannier Tanks with a wider route availability than the standard 5700 Class. These were known as the 1600 Class and were intended to replace older locomotives of a similar type. Seventy were built between 1949 and 1955 under the auspices of British Railways, which gave them the distinction of being the last of the pre-nationalisation designs to be built.

Unlike the related 5700 Class, the 1600s were devoid of any route restrictions and became employed on light shunting and branch line work. Owing to the onset of dieselisation however, their life was destined to be very short and scrapping commenced in 1959.

It is interesting to compare their dimensions with those of the 5700s.

	1600 Class	5700 Class
Cylinders (2)	$16\frac{1}{2}'' \times 24''$	$17\frac{1}{2}'' \times 24''$
Driving Wheels	$4' 1\frac{1}{2}''$ diameter	$4' 7\frac{1}{2}''$ diameter
Boiler Pressure	165 lb per sq in.	200 lb per sq in.
Weight	41 tons	48 tons

As the illustration clearly indicates, one of the 1600 Class is preserved on the Dart Valley Railway.

B.R. Standard Britannia 4–6–2

Pl. 81, 85, 88

B.R.'s first design appeared in 1951 and came in the form of these impressive Pacifics. It was the original intention to construct the

Britannias in large numbers but owing to B.R.'s change in motive power policy only 55 were built. In common with all the subsequent B.R. engines, the Britannias were built for simplicity, ease of maintenance and economy – hence the incorporation of such characteristics as 2 cylinders, high running plate for accessibility, self cleaning smokeboxes, rocking grates, self emptying ashpans and roller bearings.

Their principal statistics were: cylinders 20″ × 28″, boiler pressure 250 lb per sq in., driving wheels 6′ 2″ and an adequate grate area of 42 sq feet. They proved to be a very free running design and were capable of generating considerable power. The class had a fascinating series of names which included Writers, Poets, Military Celebrities, Heroes, early G.W. engines and Scottish Firths.

The first series were drafted on to the ex-G.E. main lines and it was from these routes that the class's fame spread. Twenty-three were allocated to Stratford and Norwich depots for working the Liverpool Street to Cambridge and Norwich expresses, they ran the latter in 2 hours. They were regarded by the G.E. enginemen as the finest engines ever built, for prior to receiving the Britannias they had used nothing larger than far less powerful 4-6-0 types.

Other express duties included the S.R.'s *Golden Arrow* boat train and the *Irish Mail* between London and Holyhead. A number of the class were used on the ex-M.R. main line between St Pancras and Manchester and some speeds of 100 m.p.h. were recorded behind them between Bedford and Luton. The class was later taken off this route however, owing to their being unsuited to the mechanical stresses involved in working over the Peak District between Derby and Manchester.

Surprising as it may seem, B.R. decided to make further tests with Westinghouse Brakes and two Britannias, Nos. 70043/4, were fitted with Westinghouse Pumps in addition to the normal vacuum apparatus. These trials were carried out on the Midland Region with air-braked mineral trains.

The first withdrawal took place in 1965 and with one exception the entire class had gone by the end of 1967. This exception was 70013 *Oliver Cromwell* which was extensively used on enthusiasts' rail-tours over the final months of steam and it actually took part in the working of the last steam train on 11 August 1968. Our illustration on plate no. 88 shows the engine at Lostock Hall after working this train, preparing to make the journey to Norwich and thence to its preservation home at Bressingham Hall near Diss.

Ex-G.C. 04 2-8-0   Pl. 11

For some 50 years this class was a familiar sight around the Nottinghamshire and Yorkshire Coalfields. They constituted the second British 2-8-0 type and first came out in 1911 to a design by John Robinson, C.M.E. of the Great Central, upon which they were classified 8K. The Great Central handled large quantities of coal traffic and, by 1913, 127 of these supreme engines were at work. Their numbers suddenly mushroomed, however, upon the outbreak of the first world war when the type was chosen by the Railway Operating Division (R.O.D.) of the British Army. Over 500 were subsequently built, many having come from private works such as North British, Robert Stephenson and Kitsons.

During the course of wartime activity they spread as far abroad as Iraq and Egypt and a large number of them worked along the Western Front in France where they hauled immense supply and troop trains. For such emergency work they received Westinghouse Air Pumps and steam heating connections.

Leading proportions were: 2 cylinders 21″ × 26″, boiler pressure of 180 lb per sq in., driving wheel diameter 4′ 8″ and a total coupled wheelbase of 25′ 5″. Their tenders held 6 tons of coal and 4,000 gallons of water.

When the war finished it was found to be impossible to sell the surplus quantities abroad because the Germans had been obliged to make full reparations in the form of locomotives and accordingly large quantities of the R.O.D.s were returned to England and stored. Eventually sales began to take place and 30 were purchased by the L.N.W.R. and 100 by the G.W.R. The former's examples had all been withdrawn by 1932 but the G.W. retained some of theirs until the 1960s. One batch was purchased for use in Australia where a few still remain at work.

The majority, however, became absorbed into the L.N.E.R. system between 1924 and 1929 upon which they became a leading freight type performing such arduous duties as the Annersley to Woodford coal hauls. During the second world war 92 were again called up for foreign service – some of these were World War I veterans – and again reached the Middle East.

In 1944 Edward Thompson, C.M.E. of the L.N.E.R., decided to rebuild them as part of his standardisation plan. Accordingly many 04s received identical boilers and cylinders to Thompson's B1 Class, outside Walschaerts valve gear, and side window cabs. This rebuild completely changed their appearance and all of the old G.C. character disappeared. The rebuilds were classified 01. Fortunately not all were so treated and some remained in the original condition until scrapping commenced in 1959.

The locomotive featured in the picture was withdrawn in 1963 and is one of the original G.C. engines as opposed to those commissioned by the R.O.D. After being stored in a derelict condition at Stratford it arrived at Leicester in December 1967 for eventual inclusion in the Museum of Technology. In November 1968 local enthusiasts commenced restoration work on behalf of the Museum authorities.

The Thompson rebuilds, along with other variants, became extinct during the 1960s.

Ex-L.N.E.R. V2 2–6–2 {Pl. 11}

For many years a classic phrase came to mind when one thought of the Gresley V2s – the engines that won the war. An exaggeration perhaps, but it does bear testimony to the magnificent feats of haulage that they performed. The design was to an excellent formula despite it being the only important British tender engine to have a 2–6–2 wheel arrangement. Their brilliance came from the combination of a wide firebox enabled by the trailing axle, a boiler of adequate dimensions, six coupled wheels for adhesion and 3 cylinders. The leading measurements were cylinders $18\frac{1}{2}''$ × 26″, 6′ 2″ diameter driving wheels, a 220 lb per sq in. boiler pressure and a grate area of no less than $41\frac{1}{4}$ sq feet.

At the time of the V2s inception in 1936 the L.N.E.R. had a crack London to Scotland freight service which left London daily at 3.35 p.m. This and other fast freights carried the specially-labelled 'Green Arrow' express parcels traffic and for publicity reasons were known as the 'Green Arrow' service. The V2s were intended to operate this traffic and although the original intention was to produce the class in a black livery it was felt that after naming the first engine *Green Arrow* the incorporation of a green livery would gain even more publicity.

As a result of this the class has always been known since as the Green Arrows. Some later engines bore the names of regiments and public schools.

A total of 184 were eventually constructed and became used on main line duties over the L.N.E.R. system, expertly handling express passenger trains as well as the heavy fitted freight. Speeds in the 90s were not uncommon and their haulage capacity may be remembered by the ability to run at 60 m.p.h. on level track with 700 tons behind the tender. Furthermore during the wartime emergencies many of them often worked expresses up to 22 coaches in length!

An interesting aspect of their career came in the 1950s when the S.R.'s Merchant Navy Class was temporarily withdrawn for detail modification and a batch of V2s were sent to cover their work. This included working such turns as the Pullman Car *Bournemouth Belle*.

In common with other Gresley designs the V2s had that engineer's conjugated valve gear and when this became worn due to high mileages the 3-cylinder exhaust beats produced fascinating rhythms.

In 1962 the first ones were withdrawn and *Green Arrow* the subject of our picture was amongst them. By 1966 the Class was a memory. Fortunately *Green Arrow* was returned to Doncaster and overhauled for preservation and after being stored at Hellifield for some years it was presented by B.R. for incorporation into the Leicester Museum of Technology.

Although officially a museum exhibit it is very possible that she will be steamed on certain occasions, but even more exciting is the hope that if the Great Central Main Line Preservation Trust succeed in their plans, then *Green Arrow* may yet return to main line service, as a permanently operational museum exhibit.

Walschaerts Valve Gear   Pl. 12, 13

This fascinating mechanism has been a delight to locomotive lovers for many years and is by far the most common type in modern steam locomotive practice. A locomotive valve-gear has to fulfil these principal functions:

1) It must enable steam to enter and leave the cylinder at the correct time during the piston travel.
2) It must permit the entry of steam to be varied by the driver.
3) It must enable the engine to be reversed.

Walschaerts gear was invented in 1844 by a Belgian engineer of that name.

D.B. 043/044 Classes 2–10–0

Pl. 15, 33–5, 41–5, 49, 51,
74–5, 79–80, 94–6, 98–100

In 1926 the first of the heavy freight engines were produced under the D.R.B.'s locomotive standardisation plan. They were the 3-cylinder 2–10–0s of Class 44, and possessed a boiler similar to that of the 01 Pacifics of the previous year. Owing to certain experiments with other 2–10–0s only 10 44s were originally constructed but in 1936 it was decided to perpetuate the class which resulted in almost 2,000 being built by 1945.

During the war the type was built and used in occupied countries and 100 of those constructed in French locomotive works passed into S.N.C.F. stock and became their Class 150X. After the war many inevitably passed to the D.R. who continued to build to the same design up to 1949. Despite their wanderings a vast quantity were inherited by the D.B. for which they still remain as a standard heavy freight design.

In 1955 the D.B. began to experiment with oil-firing and 32 of the class were converted whilst some of the coal burners received mechanical stokers. Under a renumbering scheme the oil burners became classified 043 and the coal burners 044.

They are to be found at work all over Germany and have become largely responsible for some of the magnificent work that the D.B. obtains from steam power today. These locomotives are easily capable of hauling 2,000 ton trains on level track at 40 m.p.h. A 3-cylinder 2–10–0 hard at work is a fine sight for any enthusiast but when – as frequently happens – two of the class are employed on trains of 3,000 odd tons then one begins to understand the majesty of steam.

Principal dimensions are Cylinders (3) $21\frac{1}{2}''$ × 26″, boiler pressure 228 lb per sq in. and driving wheel diameter 4′ 7″.

It is expected that they will remain in service until 1975.

B.R. Standard 4MT 4–6–0 75000

Pl. 24, 53, 62, 81–3, 90, 139

Two B.R. 4–6–0 designs were produced in 1951 and this class was the smaller of the two. By 1957 80 locomotives had been constructed. As with many of the B.R. types they were based on previous designs by the L.M.S. and in this instance the boiler was similar to that on the Class 4 2–6–4Ts. The 75000s were generally distributed and their rather compact neatness of outline rendered them popular with enthusiasts.

Some of the more important duties undertaken by them were on the Cambrian Coast and other mid-Wales lines where they replaced the ex-G.W. Manor Class and were regularly booked to haul the Cambrian Coast Express from Shrewsbury to Aberystwyth and Pwllheli. Other principal duties included working the Liverpool portion of Scottish expresses up to Preston.

Many of the class were fitted with double chimneys and those on the Western Region were turned out in G.W. green livery. Leading dimensions were: Cylinders (2) 18″ × 28″, boiler pressure 225 lb per sq in., and driving wheels 5′ 8″.

Withdrawal commenced in 1964 and one of the last duties performed was the banking of trains over the 1 in 75 climb between Tebay and Shap summit. A few remained in service until the end of steam however, and were allocated to Carnforth, the last few survivors being purchased *en bloc* for preservation in 1968. Some preserved examples are listed on page 162.

B.R. Standard 5MT 4–6–0   Pl. 24, 30, 37–8, 58, 76, 87, 129

Prior to nationalisation the three largest companies of the Big Four had all produced excellent mixed traffic 4–6–0s and when B.R. brought out their Standard 5MTs of 1951 many railwaymen regarded them as both inferior and superfluous. This feeling was very strong on the L.M.S. sections where – with some justification – the men maintained that the new Standard design should have been their Stanier Black 5s. However, B.R.s policy was sound in that a wide interchangeability of locomotive parts was economically important and this could be achieved only by producing specially designed classes. The 73000s embodied many features and details of the Britannias. And so another class entered the G.W. Hall – L.N.E.R. B1 – L.M.S. Black 5 best British mixed traffic design controversy!

The statistics of the new engines were 2 cylinders of 19″ × 28″, boiler pressure 225 lb per sq in., driving wheels 6′ 2″ and a grate area of $28\frac{1}{2}$ sq feet. Coal and water capacities were 7 tons and 4,250 gallons respectively whilst the total weight in working order was 125 tons.

Eventually the Standard 5s overcame the prejudice by proving themselves capable of some first class running and speeds in the 90s were not unknown. Many of them were built at Derby and a total of 172 were constructed between 1951 and 1957. The first batch to come out had marvellous chime whistles, but unfortunately these were later removed in favour of the plain G.W. type that had become generally adopted.

The class undertook express services on the Midland, Scottish, Western and Southern Regions. Some of the Southern ones acquired names from withdrawn engines of the old King Arthur Class which they had replaced.

All the Standard 5s were completely fitted with roller bearings and 30 received Caprotti valve gear.

Although withdrawal commenced in 1964 they became one of the last British express passenger engines to remain in service and until 1967 shared the Waterloo – Southampton – Bournemouth – Weymouth expresses along with the S.R. Pacifics. A solitary engine, No. 73069, survived through to the end of B.R. steam. It is surprising that only one of the class was preserved and this is mentioned on page 162.

D.B. 050/052 Classes 2–10–0   Pl. 25, 27

The lighter-weight sisters of the 044 Class are these 2-cylinder 2–10–0s. First built by Henschel in 1939 the class was designed to supersede the ex-Prussian G10 0–10–0s (ex-D.B. Class 057). This replacement would involve them in work of a secondary nature and accordingly their axle loading was only 15 tons.

By 1943 the immense total of 3,159 examples had been constructed. Such a building project meant that many had to be manufactured by foreign workshops in occupied countries and owing to the events of war a large number of these never reached Germany. Some were retained by Belgium (S.N.C.B.), Poland (P.K.P.) and France, where they became the S.N.C.F. Class 150Y.

Nevertheless in 1959 the D.B. still had 2,159 and they became a subject for some interesting experiments amongst which was the fitting by Henschel of Crosti pre-heater boilers to 30 of the class. Although this achieved a 17% saving on coal consumption these engines have since disappeared.

The Köln division found that they were suitable for local workings and in 1959/60 10 were modified with reduced grate area and enlarged superheaters, and by means of a water chamber placed across the firebox a larger heating surface was created. This increased the power range by some 800 h.p., gave a fuel economy of 7% and a 45°C higher steam temperature.

Another interesting aspect on some of the class were the cabins incorporated into their tenders. This practice originated in 1954 and was developed by the Köln and Essen divisions as a result of a shortage of guards-vans. Other modifications included Heinl feed water heaters and Giesl ejectors on certain engines.

The class has proved to be highly versatile and is found today all over Germany where they may be regarded as a D.B. equivalent of Britains ex-L.M.S. 5MT 4–6–0s. Some 600 remained in traffic in 1970.

Principal dimensions: 2 cylinders $23\frac{1}{2}'' \times 26''$, boiler pressure 228 lb per sq in., and driving wheel diameter $4' 7''$.

D.B. 012 Class 4–6–2 Pl. 26, 50, 70

The forerunners of the present day D.B. 012 Class were a set of 2-cylinder Pacifics of which more than 200 were built under the D.R.B. locomotive standardisation plan between 1925 and 1938. However, due to an expanding Germany and the need for faster inter-city transit, a 3-cylinder Pacific was developed which first came out in 1939. Following the current fashion of the time some were streamlined. Their original classification was 01[10].

A sum total of 55 were built by Schwartzkopffs and were put to work on the fastest and heaviest expresses. Further locomotives were cancelled due to the outbreak of war.

After the war the entire class passed to the D.B. although one had suffered a direct bomb hit in 1943 and was eventually written off. The streamlining was removed between 1946–49 and from 1953 they received new boilers in the D.B. workshops at Braunschweig; it was during this period that some were converted to oil-firing. The Oil Burners eventually became Class 012 and the Coal Burners 011.

Some of their more important duties included working the expresses between the Ruhr and Hamburg but they have since been replaced on this route by electrification. They are the most powerful Pacifics that the D.B. has ever had with the exception of the two streamlined Class 10 Pacifics of 1956.

The adoption of T.I.A. water treatment and roller bearings has helped to put up some impressive utilisation figures which have often exceeded those of the V200 Diesel Hydraulics.

The Class has the following dimensions: Cylinders (3) $19\frac{1}{2}'' \times 26''$. Boiler pressure 228 lb per sq in., driving wheels $6' 7''$ diameter, and an axle load of 20 tons.

Some may still be found at work in Germany, especially on express trains between Munster and Norddeich.

D.B. 042 Class 2–8–2

Pl. 26, 59

Introduced in 1936, this was once an important class of locomotive, 366 having been built by Schwartzkopff by 1941 and classified 41 by the D.R.B. It was intended to build further locomotives but these were cancelled owing to the advent of world war II.

Their versatility meant that they were spread over the entire D.R.B. system and by the end of the war some 250 were in West Germany, 100 in East Germany and 15 in Poland. Some of the locomotives that remained in West Germany were rebuilt with welded boilers by the D.B., and some of these were converted from coal to oil firing. The coal burners became classified 041 and the oil burners 042.

Today only the rebuilt oil burning examples remain in service and quite a few of these are based at Rheine depot. Officially speaking the class was regarded as a freight design when built, but today they are freely employed on general mixed traffic work.

All the survivors are superheated and have 2 cylinders $20\frac{1}{2}'' \times 28\frac{1}{4}''$, 5' 3" driving wheels and a boiler pressure to 284 lb per sq in.

They are splendid machines to observe in action and it is a great shame that their ranks have become so severely depleted although a few are expected to remain in service for some time to come.

B.R. Standard 9F 2–10–0

Pl. 28

Despite some early adverse criticisms the B.R. 9Fs have gone down in history as a perfect climax to British freight locomotive design. They were the final B.R. steam engines and first appeared in 1954. Building continued up to 1960 and the class totalled 251 engines.

Apart from a few Ministry of Supply locomotives, the 9Fs were the only British 2–10–0 type and were built principally for heavy freight working. Their boiler was similar to that fitted on the Britannia class and was very free steaming. They were impressive locomotives of adequate and well proportioned dimensions and had 2 cylinders of $20'' \times 28''$, a boiler pressure of 250 lb per sq in., 5' 0" diameter driving wheels and a grate area of 40·2 sq feet. Their total weight in full working order was 140 tons.

In common with most of the B.R. standards, the 9Fs were widely distributed and some of their heavier duties included the Toton to Brent and Annesley to Woodford coal trains and the famous Tyne Dock to Consett iron ore trains. The versatility of the design led to their being used on some passenger trains and it soon became apparent that they had a fine capacity for high speed running, for one reached 90 m.p.h. on the East Coast main line whilst another was recorded at 85 m.p.h. near Loughborough. One gains the impression that certain drivers enjoyed putting them through their paces but such high speed running was severely clamped down upon by the authorities. Notwithstanding this, they continued to do a certain amount of passenger work including the *Master Cutler* between Leicester and Marylebone on the ex-G.C. route and on the ex-S.D.J.R. between Bath and Templecombe.

During their relatively short existence some very interesting trials were carried out with various members of the class. One of these was on behalf of Derby Research Station who used two of them double-headed on high speed brake tests at a time when considerations were being given to automatically coupled brakes. These tests were in connection with an attempt to avoid the manual coupling up of fitted freight trains in sidings.

One member of the class, No. 92079, was used for banking duties over the 1 in 37 Lickey Incline on the Birmingham to Bristol route where it replaced the old M.R.s 0-10-0 'Big Bertha'.

Ten of those allocated to Wellingborough received Franco-Crosti boilers which increased thermal efficiency by pre-heating the feed water. In order to do this a supplementary boiler was slung beneath the main one, through which the exhaust steam from the cylinders passed. This system, which is widely used in Italy, necessitates the chimney being placed on the side of the locomotive. Other experiments included the fitting of one with a Giesl ejector in 1959, some with double chimneys and even tests with automatic stokers.

It is a tragedy that these fascinating developments should have been so quickly curtailed due to the B.R. Modernisation Plan, for just four years after the last one was built scrapping of the class commenced.

B.R.s last steam locomotive was to the 9F design and was completed at Swindon in March 1960 and specially named *Evening Star*. She was finished in G.W. livery and possessed a copper capped chimney. Some preserved examples are listed on page 162.

Ex-L.M.S. 2MT 2-6-2T   Pl. 30

This class of popular 2-6-2Ts first emerged on the L.M.S. in 1946 to a design by Ivatt and was a tank engine version of his 6400 2-6-0s of the same year. Only 10 engines were built prior to nationalisation but a further 120 came out under B.R. between 1948 and 1952. After this date they were given a reincarnation in the form of the Standard 84000 2-6-2Ts. In common with the 6400s they had 2 cylinders 16″ × 24″, a 200 lb per sq in. boiler pressure and 5′ 0″ diameter driving wheels.

Their flexible wheelbase and light axle loading made them ideal for branch line duties and some of the class were fitted for push and pull operation. Although widely used on the English part of the old L.M.S. system – e.g. the restricted Conway Valley Line – many were drafted onto the Southern Region and it was from here that the last ones were withdrawn in 1967.

One of the class, No. 41272, carried a plaque in commemoration of it having been the 7000th locomotive to be built at Crewe. Two have been preserved and one of these, No. 41241, can frequently be seen operating passenger services on the Keighley and Worth Valley Railway.

B.R. Standard 4MT 2-6-0 76000   Pl. 30, 71

Once a class of 115 engines, the 76000s possessed considerable power despite an axle loading of less than 17 tons. Such facts rendered them eminently suitable for secondary workings and gave them a wide route availability. Built between 1953 and 1957, they did service principally on the Southern, North Eastern, Midland and Scottish Regions.

The class carried identical tenders to the larger 75000s and accordingly their coal and water carrying capacity was 6 tons and 3,500 gallons respectively. Leading dimensions were: 2 cylinders $17\frac{1}{2}'' \times 26''$, boiler pressure 225 lb per sq in., driving wheels $5' 3''$ and a grate area of 23 sq feet. The boilers closely followed those of Ivatt's 3000 Class of the L.M.S. upon which the design was based and it has been stated that they were perhaps better looking engines than their L.M.S. predecessors. I may add here that the B.R. Standards were generally regarded as inferior in looks to the majority of the Big Four and pre-grouping designs.

Scrapping commenced in 1964 and some of the last examples ended their days in the Bournemouth area. The class finally disappeared in 1967. To all intents and purposes they had become extinct, but in 1969 a successful attempt was made to retrieve one from the Scrapyards at Barry in South Wales.

Ex-B.R. Standard 4MT 2-6-4T 80000s   Pl. 30

One of the earliest B.R. types to emerge was this set of mixed traffic tank engines. The first one appeared in 1951 and when building finished in 1957 the Class totalled 155 engines. They were based on the Stanier/Fairburn 2-6-4Ts of the L.M.S. Anyone who remembers seeing these engines at work can hardly fail to have been impressed by their handsome and well-proportioned appearance.

In principal dimensions they were similar to their L.M.S. forerunners having 2 cylinders of $18'' \times 28''$, a boiler pressure of 225 lb per sq in., and driving wheels of a $5' 8''$ diameter. Coal-carrying capacity was $3\frac{1}{2}$ tons and water 2,000 gallons. These locomotives also had a water storage space beneath the coal bunker.

The 80000s replaced the Stanier 3-cylinder tanks on the London (Fenchurch Street) – Tilbury – Southend services, although in many areas they became intermingled with the 2-cylinder Stanier/Fairburn locomotives. They were widely used on the Southern region in the Brighton, Tunbridge Wells and Dover areas. Other duties included suburban workings from St Pancras and Marylebone, whilst large numbers worked in Scotland, mainly in the Glasgow and Edinburgh districts.

Many of the class had a very short working life owing to the rapid progress made in the modernisation of suburban services, and as early as July 1967 all had been withdrawn. The last survivors were all at Bournemouth and one of these is featured in our picture.

Some preserved examples are mentioned on page 162 one of which was rescued from Woodhams of Barry at a scrap price of £3,000. In 1969 a new scheme was commenced to save a third example – again from the derelict batch at Woodhams.

Ex-S.R. Unrebuilt West Country Class 4-6-2   Pl. 67
Ex-S.R. Rebuilt West Country Class 4-6-2   Pl. 33, 40, 63-4, 72-3
Ex-S.R. Rebuilt Merchant Navy Class 4-6-2   Pl. 39, 77

Because these locomotives have such a close family history they have been grouped together under one heading for convenience.

Prior to O.V.S. Bulleid succeeding Maunsell as C.M.E. of the S.R. he had been assistant to Gresley on the L.N.E.R. At the time of Bulleid's succession the Southern Railway was in need of larger locomotives for its many important express duties, including the boat trains between London and Dover, Folkestone and Southampton, and the longer West Country main line runs down to Exeter and onwards to Plymouth. Many of the bridges that had prevented the use of larger engines in the past had been strengthened and accordingly the authorities expressed a need for a passenger locomotive capable of hauling 500 ton trains at 70 m.p.h.

Gresley's big-engine conception may be seen in Bulleid's subsequent production of an air-smoothed 3-cylinder Pacific. The new class was known as the Merchant Navies and was named after shipping companies with which the S.R. had affinity at Southampton. Due to Bulleid's incorporation of many revolutionary features the class became one of the most controversial in British locomotive history.

Some of these features were an all-welded steel firebox fitted with thermic syphons, boxpok driving wheels for greater strength special suspension arrangements, and electric lighting throughout – even under the streamlined casing. The valve spindle was driven by chains and the entire mechanism was enclosed in an oil bath in order to reduce both maintenance and wear. As an attempt to ensure adequate reserves of power within the weight restriction laid down the Merchant Navies possessed a high boiler pressure and their driving axle loading was no more than 21 tons. One of the class was originally fitted with a mechanical stoker.

The first engine emerged from Eastleigh Works in 1941 and was followed by 29 others and they proceeded to perform brilliant work on the Dover, Bournemouth and Exeter runs. One of the many surprises about the Merchant Navies was that such a revolutionary design should have been prepared under wartime conditions. In June 1945 a smaller version was produced for the S.R.s secondary lines. These were called the Light Pacifics having a driving axle weight of only $18\frac{3}{4}$ tons. Initially they were built for the routes west of Exeter and accordingly the first engine was named *Exeter* at that town on 10 July 1945. The class was officially known as the West Countries and they carried beautiful scroll nameplates incorporating the coats of arms of West Country towns.

Later engines of the Light series became the Battle of Britain Class and these commemorated the great feats in world war II, especially the defeat of Hitler's Luftwaffe over the south-eastern counties of England in which they were put to work. A total of 110 WC/BBs were built, the last ones emerging as late as 1950.

A comparative table of dimensions will be of interest.

	Merchant Navy	WC/BB
Cylinders	(3) $18'' \times 24''$	(3) $16\frac{1}{2}'' \times 24''$
Driving Wheel Diameter	6' 2''	6' 2''
Boiler Pressure	280 lb per sq in.*	280 lb per sq in.*
Total Weight	144 tons	130 tons

* later reduced to 250 lb per sq in.

Both classes were magnificent and their numerous exploits included such delights as the Merchant Navy that averaged 80 m.p.h. for 45 miles whilst hauling a Pullman Car express of 555 tons and the one that ran the 84 miles from Salisbury to Waterloo with a 430 ton train in 73 minutes. Furthermore, during the locomotive exchanges of 1948 one of the Light Pacifics attained a power output of over 2,000 d.b. h.p.

Despite their capabilities they had, by 1956, become far too un-orthodox for British Railways; the streamlined casing was regarded as superfluous and the oil baths were giving continual trouble owing to leakages – in fact the escape of oil had caused some serious fires. Accordingly it was decided to rebuild one of the Merchant Navies on more conventional lines. The streamlined casing, oil bath, and thermic syphons were all removed and the valve gear was converted to the traditional Walschaerts type. By the end of 1959 the entire class had been rebuilt. The same conversions were undertaken on the Light Pacifics but not all were completed owing to B.R.'s decision to abandon steam, and two of the original ones were still at work from Salisbury depot in 1967. These S.R. Pacifics were the last British high speed express engines to be built under private enterprise and the last to remain in service.

Many locomotive students regarded the original air-smoothed engines as plain and ugly but to me they harmonised perfectly with the soft green countryside through which they worked. I have endeavoured to show how complete the blend was in my illustration on plate 67. In their final days both types operated the Bournemouth line and attracted thousands of enthusiasts from all over Britain. The enginemen knew that they were responsible for the last runs of the British express steam tradition and – encouraged by enthusiasts – innumerable 100 m.p.h. bursts were made in 1966/7, especially over the racing ground between Basingstoke and Woking. Just before the end came one was officially logged at 103 m.p.h. with an 11-coach train, whilst another was whipped up to 105 m.p.h.

So ended Britain's express steam and within weeks of such feats being performed they were cut up in the scrapyards of South Wales.

Preserved examples are listed on page 161.

Ex-P.L.M. 231G   Pl. 36, 48, 66

One of the loveliest locomotive experiences I have had was to see these magnificent French Pacifics in action, for they possessed a power and majesty that were like no other locomotive. It is small wonder that the French enginemen knew them as 'Les Belles Machines'. Originally these locomotives were the P.L.M. 231D/231F Class and were built between 1922 and 1925. They were one of many classes of 4-cylinder compound Pacifics to work in France where the type was almost universally accepted.

Pacifics had first been introduced into Europe by the Paris-Orleans Railway in 1907; by 1910 there were 225 of them at work in the country and eventually the figure rose to 1400. The popularity of the type may be further demonstrated by the fact that in 1950 over 1,000 remained despite considerable advances in electrification.

The 231Gs came into being when the great French engineer André Chapelon of the P-O influenced the rebuilding of the P.L.M.'s 231D/Fs. This was carried out between 1934 and 1948 and 193 of the original locomotives were so treated. The engines were greatly improved by the rebuilding which included raising the degree of superheating, modifications to the blast pipe, and improvements in the design of the steam passages. Other features were the fitting of double chimneys, ACFI feed water heaters and the replacement of slide valves by piston valves on the inside cylinders. After rebuilding they were capable of generating 3,000 i.h.p. compared with the previous 2,000 i.h.p.

The principal dimensions were 4 cylinders; High Pressure (2) $17\frac{1}{2}''$ × $25\frac{1}{2}''$, Low Pressure (2) $25\frac{1}{2}''$ × $25\frac{1}{2}''$. Boiler pressure 230 lb per sq in., and a driving wheel diameter of 6' 7".

Amongst their exploits were such performances as Paris to Marseilles, 536 miles – average speed 60 m.p.h. hauling 400 tons. In later years modernisation forced them away from their original system and in the 1950s some were drafted on to the old Nord main line from Calais to Amiens over which they worked such expresses as the Golden Arrow. Their duties on the Nord were shared by other French Pacifics including a close relation, the 231K (ex-P.L.M. Class 231C) which was almost identical in appearance.

The 231Gs remained on the Nord until the summer of 1969 when they were replaced by diesels. By this time the class had become the last of the French Pacifics and their passing ended a tradition of over 60 years, and what was to many the epitomy of beauty and power became just a memory.

In 1970 the hearts of enthusiasts the continent over were gladdened by the arrival in Britain of a 231K for preservation. She has been delivered to the Lakeside Railway depot at Carnforth. Other Pacifics are preserved in France.

S.N.C.F. 141R   Pl. 46–8

During World War II the French National Railways suffered incredible damage and at the time of the liberation only 3,000 of their 17,000 pre-war locomotives were in a serviceable condition. Such a state of affairs was the result of sabotage during the German occupation, allied bombardments and destruction wrought by the retreating enemy. Further to this many locomotives had been taken away by the Germans for use in other countries.

A state of emergency existed and as a stopgap, some British and American locomotives and rolling stock were supplied. As France and the Allies worked to restore the shattered railway system it became obvious that many new locomotives would be required as only some 5,600 locomotives were in working order by the beginning of 1945.

France appealed to America for assistance and it was agreed that new locomotives must be supplied. In December 1944 a group from the French Railway Mission went to Baldwins Locomotive Works in Philadelphia to discuss the new design and the decision was made for a 2–8–2 mixed-traffic type to be built, capable of hauling trains of 800 tons weight on level track at 65 m.p.h. In addition one of the chief considerations was that they should be completely reliable and easy to maintain. Construction began in March 1945, and so were born the famous 141Rs.

They were a 2-cylinder design of $23\frac{1}{2}''$ × 28" dimensions, with a boiler pressure of 220 lb per sq in., and driving wheels of 5' 5" diameter. Great care was taken in both design and building and they proved to be magnificent machines in every way.

On 3 November 1945 the first 4 of the class arrived in France with great ceremony. The initial locomotive 141R 1 carried the name *Liberation* and thus the class has often been known since. They were very well received by the French enginemen and as more locomotives arrived from America so the 141Rs spread throughout France. Their original black livery eventually gave way to the S.N.C.F. olive green on certain regions.

A total of 1,340 were shipped to France between 1945 and 1947 although only 1,323 arrived, 17 of the class being lost at sea en route. Of those constructed in the U.S.A. a combined total of 1,200 came from the works of Baldwin, Lima and ALCO. The remaining 140 were built in Canada by the Montreal Locomotive Works and the Canadian Locomotive Works. Of those delivered to the S.N.C.F. 604 were oil burners and 719 were coal-fired and many of the latter had mechanical stokers. Other attributes included feed water heaters, Timken roller bearings and steam-powered reversing gear.

Since those troubled times the 141Rs have become a part of French locomotive history and for years they were a familiar sight all over France. Encroaching modernisation has unfortunately seriously depleted their ranks and recently hundreds have been found rusting away in locomotive dumps and scrapyards all over the country.

Fortunately, however, some still remain at work – as thoroughly capable and reliable as ever. In fact they are responsible for the vast bulk of the remaining S.N.C.F. steam workings. The class will remain until the cessation of steam power. As late as March 1970 one of them deputised for a failed diesel and worked the *Golden Arrow* express between Calais and Amiens, it kept time perfectly!

They have always been a controversial type amongst railway enthusiasts, especially those who prefer the more distinctive designs of the French tradition but everyone is united in the hope that at least one of the Liberations will be preserved.

Ex-G.W.R. 4500 Class 2–6–2T   Pl. 55

This Churchward Design of 1906 provided the G.W.R. with an excellent set of mixed duty tank engines for cross country and branch line work. Quite a number of the G.W.R's secondary routes were both curved and steeply graded and it was on such lines that the 4500s triumphed. They were sufficiently powerful to handle considerable loads whilst their short wheel base combined with the pony trucks on both leading and trailing axles gave them a wide route availability. They replaced many old and smaller G.W. tank types.

Between 1906 and 1929, 175 were built and for over 60 years were a characteristic feature of West Country rural life. Instead of the traditional G.W. copper cap chimney the 4500s possessed a plain cast iron type despite which they remained as one of the most delightful engines to behold on the system. This fact clearly indicated that there was more to the aesthetics of G.W. design than the mere adornment of copper cap chimneys. The 4500s contrasted with the other leading design of G.W. passenger tank, the 5100s/6100s, in that they had 4' 7½" driving wheels as opposed to 5' 8". Other principal dimensions were 2 cylinders 17" × 24" and 200 lb per sq in. boiler pressure.

132

Scrapping commenced in 1950 and by the mid 1960s the class had disappeared. Upon withdrawal in 1963 one of them, No. 4555, was purchased by Mr Patrick Whitehouse, a leading railway preservationist and author. The engine now works on the Dart Valley Railway, as illustrated.

Ex-G.W.R. 1400 Class 0–4–2T   Pl. 56

When one considers the vintage character of the 1400 Class it is hard to believe that they were only built as recently as 1932–36. Having said this however, it must be stated that the class was specifically produced to replace a similar type of locomotive which dated back to the 1870s.

The 1400s became a very pleasant feature of G.W. country branch lines and the majority of the class were fitted with push and pull apparatus for working Auto trains. The Auto trains were usually of small formation and there was a driver's compartment at the front of the coach situated at the opposite end from the engine. A mechanical gear coupled this coach with the locomotive's controls and thereby avoided the need for the engine to run round to the other end of the train when changing direction. The fireman remained on the locomotive footplate and was joined by the driver only when the set was running engine first. These may be regarded as a form of predecessor of today's diesel railcars. A complete Auto-train set is preserved on the Dart Valley Railway and may frequently be seen in operation.

The 1400s were of lightweight construction – 41 tons only – which gave them freedom to work over the most restricted of country branches. A total of 95 engines were built and these fell into two sections:

1400 – 1474 Auto fitted, built between 1932 – 1936 (Originally numbered 4800s)

5800 – 5819 For ordinary branch operation, built between 1932 – 1933

The closure of branch lines and advent of diesel railcars accelerated their demise and by the mid 1960s they had disappeared.

Understandably quite a number have been preserved but the best place to see one is, of course, on the Dart Valley Railway.

Ex-L.N.E.R. A4 4–6–2   Pl. 57, 61

Here is one of the most sought-after classes by enthusiasts the world over. For almost 30 years these wonderful engines were responsible for the crack expresses on the East Coast main line from Kings Cross to Scotland. They were named after animals, wild birds, dominions, statesmen and L.N.E.R. company chairmen. One of the class, *Mallard,* holds the world speed record for steam traction of 126 m.p.h. which it achieved with a special 240-ton train in 1938. Another locomotive of the same type, *Silver Fox,* holds the British steam speed record, for a train carrying fare-paying passengers, of 113 m.p.h.

It is impossible to list the A4s' attainments in so short a space but I cannot resist mentioning the *Silver Jubilee* trip when 100 m.p.h. was maintained for 43 miles and 91 m.p.h. averaged for over 70 miles. During the run, the engine averaged $108\frac{1}{2}$ m.p.h. for the 10 miles between Biggleswade and St Neots in Huntingdonshire.

As late as the 1960s, the A4s were still performing brilliant work. One of their duties being the *Elizabethan* Kings Cross to Edinburgh service and they ran the 393 miles non-stop at an average speed of 60 m.p.h. This service, it may be noted, often involved loads of 425 tons!

In 1963 in the shadow of modernisation they became displaced from the more important duties and a few survivors were banished to Scotland where they were put on to the Glasgow to Aberdeen expresses. These remaining engines were eventually replaced by diesels in 1966.

The locomotive illustrated is named after its designer *Sir Nigel Gresley* and was his 100th Pacific. The engine was named by the L.N.E.R. chairman William Whitelaw during a special ceremony at Marylebone Station on 26 November 1937.

The leading dimensions of the A4 Class are: 3 cylinders $18\frac{1}{2}'' \times 26''$, a boiler pressure of 250 lb per sq in., driving wheels 6' 8'' diameter and a grate area of $41\frac{1}{4}$ sq ft. Total weight is 168 tons. One of the features that made these engines so successful was the internal streamlining of the steam passages.

Their universal appeal is manifested in the fact that no fewer than 6 out of the original 34 have been preserved, two of which have gone to America. It is the ardent hope of the preservation movement that if sufficient suitable track can be found, Britain will once again have the joy of seeing and hearing one of these magnificent engines in action.

B.R. Standard 3MT 2-6-0 77000   Pl. 65

These Standard 3MTs comprised one of the smallest B.R. Standard Classes. Only 20 engines were built, all of them in 1954. As the illustration shows they were a diminutive design and were intended to have a high route availability upon services of a secondary nature. It was proposed to build further locomotives of the class but these were cancelled before construction began.

Their 2 cylinders were $17\frac{1}{2}'' \times 26''$, boiler pressure 200 lb sq in. and driving wheels 5' 3'' diameter.

The entire class was to be found on the N.E. and Scottish Regions. For some years they worked the ex-N.E.R. Cross Pennine route between Tebay and Barnard Castle and also the Alston branch on the Cumberland/Northumberland border.

During the 1960s one of the class, No. 77014 – the subject of our picture – wandered onto the Southern Region and in so doing managed to outlive all of its sister engines. For some time it worked from Guildford Depot although its final duties involved the working of empty stock trains between Bournemouth and Branksome Carriage Sidings. It finally disappeared in July 1967.

They were in no way an influential class and were permitted to pass to extinction.

Ex-L.M.S. Jinty 0-6-0T   Pl. 68

After the formation of the L.M.S. in 1923 it was quickly realised that the new company desperately needed some general duty shunting engines for their numerous freight yards. L.M.S. policy at that time was to perpetuate the old Midland Railway's designs and accordingly the type chosen became based on a Johnson Class of 1899 of which only 60 engines had been constructed. The new L.M.S. engines became known as Jintys and over 400 were built between 1924 and 1931. Many of these came from private builders including Bagnall and Hunslet.

The class was widely distributed over the English part of the L.M.S. system and even the smallest of freight yards invariably possessed at least one of them. They were highly successful and very affectionately regarded by the enginemen. So suitable were they, in fact, that the War Department acquired some for overseas service prior to their commissioning the Hunslet Austerities.

During the war a couple were converted to 5' 3" gauge and sent to Ireland where they worked as station pilots at Belfast. As a result of enemy action some were lost at sea and amongst those that did return after the war was one that bore the chimney of a Dean Goods 0-6-0 – presumably the foreign engineers had no eye for the family backgrounds of British locomotives!

Not all of them were confined to shunting duties and some, allocated to Devons Road depot in Bow, had vacuum brakes fitted for working passenger trains between Fenchurch St. and High Barnet. Jintys were also found at important main line stations where they were employed on empty stock workings.

The engines were 31' long, had 2 cylinders of 18" × 26" dimensions and driving wheels of 4' 7" diameter.

Scrapping commenced in 1959 and proceeded rapidly as the class became replaced by diesel shunters; by 1967 the last had disappeared from B.R. Fortunately, however, this was not quite the end, for one of them, No. 47445, was purchased by the N.C.B. and put to work at Crigglestone Colliery in Yorkshire where it received an orange livery and red side rods. The engine has been purchased by Derby Corporation.

Another preserved example is listed on page 160.

B.R. Standard 2MT 2-6-0 78000   Pl. 68

The smallest tender locomotives in the B.R. range were this class of 65 engines built between 1953 and 1956. Their boilers were virtually identical to those of the L.M.S. 6400 Ivatt 2-6-0s upon which the class was based. In common with other B.R. designs they possessed such modern devices as manually-operated blow down valves for the discharge of sludge, self-cleaning smokeboxes, rocking grates, and self-emptying ashpans. Their tenders were fitted with roller bearings.

Principal dimensions were: Cylinders (2) $16\frac{1}{2}" \times 24"$, boiler pressure 200 lb per sq in., and driving wheel diameter 5' 0". The class was designed to have a wide route availability in order for them to replace older 0-6-0 types on secondary branch line duties.

Two of the class Nos. 78013/28 were modified at Crewe in 1964 with cut-down cabs to enable them to work coal traffic on the old Leicester and Swannington Railway's route between Coalville and Leicester. This line which included the notoriously narrow mile-long Glenfield Tunnel (built 1832) had for years been operated by ancient ex-M.R. 2F 0-6-0s since they were the only suitable type that could pass through it.

The class was widely distributed when withdrawal commenced in 1963 and in May 1967 they became extinct after the last ones had worked out their days as station pilots at Preston. No examples have been preserved although one of the similar ex-L.M.S. 6400s may be found at the Lakeside Railway's depot at Carnforth.

D.B. 023 Class 2-6-2   Pl. 78

The actual forerunners of this class were two locomotives constructed in 1941 as the beginning of a standard type for the D.R.B. However, after world war II these locomotives passed into D.R. stock and the D.B. produced their own similar design in 1950 which became the 023 Class.

A total of 105 were constructed by 4 different builders between 1950 and 1959 as a result of which some detail differences occur especially in boiler construction and axle weights – which vary between 17 and 19 tons. Some members of the class are fitted with roller bearings.

This standard design was intended to replace the old Prussian P8 4-6-0s (D.B. 038 Class) a type that dates back to 1906. The replacement would certainly have been completed were it not for the fact that owing to modernisation programmes on the D.B. the building of the 023 was cut short. This has led to a situation today whereby both the 023s and 038s can be seen at work side by side. The intention now, of course, is eventually to replace both types with diesel or electric locomotives.

No. 23·105 was the last steam engine to be built for the D.B. being completed on 6.12.59. The class is mainly employed on secondary passenger workings for which some are push-and-pull fitted.

The principal dimensions are as follows: 2-cylinders $21\frac{1}{2}'' \times 26''$, boiler pressure 228 lb per sq in. and driving wheels of 5' 9'' diameter.

Undoubtedly the 023s will be amongst the last steam engines to remain in West Germany despite some of the enginemen still preferring the old P8s. They are widely distributed but may be seen especially at Saarbrücken, Kaiserslautern and Crailsheim.

D.B. Stop Signal   Pl. 97

German signalling is similar to the British in that the 'block system' is used. The signals illustrated are 'stop' semaphores and are a direct equivalent of the British home signal. These indicate that the train must stop when the arm is horizontal but may proceed when it is raised at 45°. At night a red light is displayed for the stop position and a green one for the all clear, the lights are situated beside the post just beneath the arm.

Hudswell Clarke 0-6-0ST   Pl. 101
Hudswell, Clarke and Co. Ltd, Railway Foundry, Leeds

Hudswell Clarke are situated at the Jacks Lane Works, Hunslet on part of the site originally occupied by the old Railway Foundry which was established in 1839 and partially demolished in 1859. It was here in 1860 that Hudswell Clarke built their works and situated on the same original site was Hunslet Engine Co., Manning Wardle and Kitsons. The area has become known as the Railway Foundry Estate.

Hudswell Clarke have had over 100 years in dealing with steam locomotives and for long have been one of the leading locomotive builders in the country. Their last steam engine was built in 1961 although they continued to do repairs until 1968. Today they remain as one of the few private locomotive builders and are actively engaged in building diesels for industrial use.

The locomotive pictured is one of many that worked in the ironstone fields and is to a design of adequate dimension that dates back to the turn of the century. This particular example was photographed at Cranford and was one of the last of its type to remain. It was broken up c. 1966. No examples of the class have been preserved.

Robert Stephenson 0-6-2T   Pl. 102
Kitson 0-6-2T   Pl. 103

Robert Stephenson & Co. Ltd, Darlington, Kitson & Co., Airedale Foundry, Leeds

These were the famous 0-6-2Ts from Philadelphia, and one of the last truly vintage designs to remain at work in Britain. The Kitson locomotives dated back to 1904 whilst the similar yet larger Robert Stephenson examples were of 1909 vintage.

For many years they did heavy duties on one of the largest colliery networks in Britain. The system, originally the Lambton Collieries, was situated 5 miles S.W. of Sunderland on land owned by the Earl of Durham, and as early as 1860 had a total of 70 miles of railway track. After an amalgamation the company extended even further and became known as Lambton, Hetton and Joicey Collieries.

In the later days the engine sheds for the system were situated at a small mining village named Philadelphia which became a Mecca for steam enthusiasts and was widely noted for its ancient locomotives. One stored there in 1969 actually dated back to 1846! Another distinction was the systems use of 0-6-0 tender engines the last of which was a Lambton built veteran of 1877. It remained the last tender engine in British industrial use until its withdrawal in 1966.

The 0-6-2s regularly hauled coal trains between Penshaw and Lambton Staiths on the River Wear at Sunderland. It was for this duty that the cabs had to be cut down in size to enable them to pass through the narrow tunnel that led to the Staithes. This modification did little to enhance what was otherwise an extremely handsome tank engine. One of the Kitsons acquired an American locomotive whistle from Philadelphia, U.S.A., and, as can be imagined, this was especially thrilling to hear.

After 1929 further 0-6-2s were purchased from the Great Western. These dated back to the 1890s and originated on the Taff Vale Railway and had, of course, passed into G.W. stock at the grouping. This fact is very interesting because it gave the colliery system three completely different designs of 0-6-2T engine, all of which looked very similar.

Philadelphia was also famous for its North Durham area workshops known as Lambton Works, and in 1967 two of the 0-6-2Ts were completely overhauled there. This raised hopes amongst the locomotive fraternity that despite dieselisation and a reduction in the collieries' output some of them would remain in service for a number of years to come. Unfortunately this did not take place and in 1969 the last example was withdrawn. The system completely dispensed with steam power a few months later.

Some of the 0–6–2Ts are still lying derelict at Philadelphia and it is hoped that at least one can be saved for preservation.

Hunslet Austerity 0–6–0ST   Pl.104, 107, 109

Including Locomotives built by The Hunslet Engine Company, Hunslet, Leeds; W. Bagnall and Robert Stephenson & Hawthorn.

Leeds has for long had a great locomotive building tradition and it is possible that more locomotives have been built there than any other city in Britain. This achievement is in no small way due to the Hunslet Engine Company who, apart from having produced vast quantities of locomotives for British use, have also exported all over the world. The company was formed in 1864 as J. T. Leather and took the name Hunslet Engine Co. in 1872.

In 1943 it was announced that the Ministry of Supply had placed an order with one of the larger locomotive manufacturing companies for some 0–6–0STs of a simple and robust design based on that company's standard shunting type. The company proved to be Hunslet of Leeds and the type referred to was their 18″ × 26″ cylinder 50550 Class of 1941.

At the Ministry of Supply conference it had been suggested that the L.M.S. Jinty 0–6–0T design would fulfil all requirements but Edgar Alcock, Hunslet's Chairman, convinced the Ministry in favour of his 18″ saddle tank. He claimed that Hunslet's locomotives were of a more straightforward design which rendered them emminently suitable for rapid production and furthermore that the shorter wheelbase would give his locomotives a greater route availability.

It was at this time that military operations in Europe were progressing and versatile locomotives were urgently needed. The matter finally became decided when it was realised that Hunslet's engines would be fully capable of meeting the M.O.S. requirements from a power point of view which were
1) The ability to start 1,100 ton trains on level track
2) The ability to start   550 ton trains on 1 in 100 gradient
3) The ability to start   300 ton trains on 1 in 50 gradient

Accordingly on 1 January 1943 the first of the Hunslet Austerities – as they became known – emerged from the Works and by 1945 150 had been built, many having been commissioned from other builders. Amongst these were Andrew Barclay, W. Bagnall, Hudswell Clark, Robert Stephenson and Hawthorn and the Vulcan Foundry. Thus was born one of Britain's more numerous designs and one that was eventually to become a tradition of its own among industrial locomotives. Over the next 20 years a total of 484 were built.

It is interesting to observe the family background of these famous engines which is summarised by the following table:

	Type	Cyls. (2, Inside)	Boiler Pressure	Driving Wheel Diameter	Purpose
Hunslet Design 1923	0–6–0ST	16 × 22	160	3′ 9″	Standard Design
Hunslet Design 1937	0–6–0ST 48150 Class	18 × 26	170	4′ 0½″	Specially built for GKB of Cardiff
Hunslet Design 1941	0–6–0ST 50550 Class	18 × 26	170	4′ 0½″	Specially built for Stewarts & Lloyds of Corby
Hunslet Design 1943	0–6–0ST	18 × 26	170	4′ 3″	Special development for the Ministry of Supply

The weight of the Austerity Tanks is 48 tons.

Once in traffic they proved to be excellent performers and were especially free in steaming. In addition to going abroad some were put to work in Army Depots and Governmental establishments all over the country. The ending of the war found them scattered throughout Europe and many were destined never to return, some being retained by France and even North Africa. In 1946 the L.N.E.R. purchased 75 from the M.O.S. for shunting duties and classified them J94, whilst many others were sold to the National Coal Board where they became one of the standard types, being put to work at collieries throughout Great Britain. In fact the N.C.B. were so satisfied with them that they continued to order new ones until 1964 – despite encroaching dieselisation!

Their passing into public ownership resulted in many of the class being named and also to their appearance in several liveries, notably black, red, blue, green and yellow. Today the type is principally associated with the N.C.B. who have fitted some with Giesl ejectors. Other modifications to certain engines have included the fitting of mechanical stokers allied to the Hunslet 'gas-producer' system together with their 'special blast pipe'. This innovation was to comply with the Clean Air Act that has been enforced in many industrial areas as it effectively controls the emission of black smoke.

Along with other 'austere' wartime designs the Hunslet Austerities, generally speaking, have been unpopular with enthusiasts. Perhaps they are not the most attractive of engines but through their supreme performances the type has done a great deal to extend the life of steam power in British industry.

Many remain in traffic today and their working existence seems assured for a few more years at least. I mention in passing that one of the Hunslet 48150 Class mentioned in the above comparative table can be seen in preserved form at Splott Park Cardiff. Preserved Austerity examples are listed on page 179.

In 1964 the Hunslet Company gained the distinction of building the last standard gauge steam locomotive for Great Britain. The engine was delivered to the N.C.B. Hunslet continue to repair steam engines and have been responsible for overhauling *Flying Scotsman* and the ex-L.M.S. Jubilee *Bahamas* after their purchase for preservation. They also handle locomotives from the Festiniog Railway.

Thus it may be said that the Company, although heavily committed to building diesels is playing an important part – albeit on a strictly commercial basis – in the preservation movement, and their willingness to retain certain plant for the overhaul of steam engines is a great consolation to locomotive owners throughout the country.

Robert Stephenson and Hawthorn 0–6–0ST
Pl. 104

Robert Stephenson & Hawthorn Co. Ltd., Darlington and Newcastle-upon-Tyne.

George Stephenson's brilliant son, Robert, commenced this company in the 1820s and large workshops were built at Newcastle. The Stephensons were very active in both early locomotive and railway development which resulted in the company becoming well established within a few years. In 1900 the company transferred its workshops to

Darlington but upon taking over the locomotive building interests of Hawthorn Leslie of Newcastle in 1937 it became re-established in that town and from then on built engines in both places. Included in the main line engines that they built were some batches of Pannier Tanks for the G.W.R. The company remained as Robert Stephenson & Hawthorn and continued to build steam designs up to the late 1950s. In 1961 they were absorbed by English Electric.

One of the most pleasant aspects of today's locomotive scene in the North East is the presence of these splendid 18″ Saddle Tanks that were built by the company during the 1940s/50s. The class has 2 cylinders of 18″ × 24″ proportions, 4′ 0″ diameter driving wheels, a boiler pressure of 180 lb per sq in. and a total weight of 53 tons.

The engines used on the Backworth, Wearmouth, Cambois and Philadelphia networks have now disappeared but others remain at Ashington. This 0-6-0ST is one of the largest locomotives still to be found at work for British industry.

Robert Stephenson and Hawthorn 0-6-0T   Pl. 105

Our illustration shows one of the two outside cylinder side tank engines that were built specially for operating passenger trains over the Ashington colliery network. Constructed in 1954 they became known locally as the 'Passenger Tanks' and worked between Hirst – Linton and Ellington until withdrawal of the service in 1966. After this date they undertook the day to day colliery freight workings along with the other engines.

The two cylinders measure 18″ × 24″, driving wheels are 4′ 6″ diameter, boiler pressure 180 lbs per sq in. and weight 55 tons.

By 1969 both had been withdrawn from service but one has been retained for possible preservation.

Bagnall 0-6-0ST   Pl. 106
W. G. Bagnall Ltd., Castle Engine Works, Stafford.

William G. Bagnall of Stafford were one of the foremost locomotive builders in Britain and as a tribute to the company one of their early locomotives now rests on a plinth in the town. Originally they commenced as agricultural implement makers and later graduated to the manufacture of locomotives. Bagnall ceased building steam engines in the mid 1950s and have since been absorbed by English Electric.

Apart from their own many designs the company is known for the building of L.M.S. Jintys, G.W.R. Pannier Tanks and some of the Hunslet Austerity type locomotives. The handsome engine illustrated was to one of Bagnall's standard designs with 16″ cylinders. The first example was built in 1934 for Birchenwood Coking Plant and the final one appeared in 1955. The class totalled only 18 engines and their distribution was as follows: 9 to the N.C.B. Staffs. Area – who later fitted 3 with Giesl ejectors – 7 to the Preston Docks Authority (as illustrated) and 1 each to the Leicestershire Area Coalfield and to Birchenwood.

A locomotive from the Preston Dock batch has been acquired by Helical Springs Ltd. Railway Preservation at Lytham St Annes, Lancs.

Hawthorn Leslie/Hudswell Clarke 0–4–0ST   Pl. 108

R. & W. Hawthorn Leslie & Co. Ltd., Forth Bank Works, Newcastle-upon-Tyne.

In view of the close similarity between the two locomotives illustrated they have been grouped together for convenience.

H.L. 0–4–0ST

The company of R. & W. Hawthorn Leslie was formed in 1886 although their locomotive building activities date well before this time, originally being known as R. & W. Hawthorn Ltd. Apart from their locomotive construction the company was also famous for shipbuilding which included Destroyers for the Royal Navy. Throughout their long history they have built a number of main line engines and perhaps the most famous was the Clan Class 4–6–0s for the Highland Railway.

The locomotive illustrated was one of their standard designs for industry, dating back to the last century and after the company's amalgamation with Robert Stephenson it was perpetuated with little more than detail variations.

Very large numbers were built and they were found in collieries, quarries, electricity stations, ship yards, breweries, cement works, docks and steel works. Many similar engines are preserved including *Asbestos* – one of 1909 vintage – by the Railway Preservation Society at Chasewater, and No. 3 of 1924 on the Foxfield Light Railway.

H.C. 0–4–0ST

One of a very long tradition of 0–4–0STs that have been built by Hudswell Clarke since the last century. The type was as generally distributed as the H. L. design mentioned above.

Similar but slightly larger engines were to be found at the Kirkstall Forge and Engineering Co., Newlay, Yorks., and in the 1960s a modern version was specially produced for the N.C.B. One of the Kirkstall Forge engines *Henry De Lacey II* is preserved on the Middleton Railway Trust, Leeds.

Ex-G.W.R. Design 1500 Class   Pl. 110

Old railway traditions died hard and this was especially true on the Great Western who seemed to take a delight in perpetuating the building of their own designs after nationalisation – a fact further borne out by their initial rejection of the B.R. Standards!

These heavy duty Pannier Tanks first appeared in 1949. Originally they were intended as a new G.W. standard class but in the event only 10 were built. The class was designed by F. W. Hawksworth for heavy shunting duties on curves of a minimum radius of 3 chains and to facilitate this the wheelbase was only 12' 10". An unusual feature of these locomotives was their outside Walschaerts valve gear. Other dimensions included 2 cylinders of $17\frac{1}{2}'' \times 24''$, boiler pressure 200 lb per sq in., and 4' $7\frac{1}{2}''$ diameter driving wheels. The outside valve gear and absence of footplating gave excellent accessibility from a maintenance viewpoint and was an indication of the time when this was becoming a vital factor.

For some years one of their principal duties was the hauling of empty stock trains in and out of Paddington Station – a duty that these sturdy little tank engines performed with ease.

By 1964 the class had disappeared from B.R. and they would have passed to extinction had it not been for the purchase of 3 of them by the National Coal Board for their Coventry Colliery. At Coventry they received a red livery but retained the original G.W. fittings and the 3 survived there until the end of 1969.

It is intended that 2 of them shall go to the Severn Valley Railway at Bridgnorth for preservation.

Robert Stephenson and Hawthorn 0–6–0ST   Pl. 111–2, 116

This 1950 design of powerful 18″ inside-cylinder engines was specially produced for the Stewarts & Lloyds Minerals systems where they became known as the 56 Class. They proved to be highly successful and were capable of hauling trains of several hundred tons out of the ironstone quarries. Frequently they would be employed on the heavier and longer distance trains upon which, by sheer virtue of their size, they showed a marked superiority over the smaller 0–6–0STs.

Of the 10 engines built 9 went to the Pen Green depot at Corby and 1 to Stewarts & Lloyds pits at Harlaxton in Lincolnshire. The Harlaxton engine was named *Achilles* and one of the Pen Green engines became *Jupiter* when it was later transferred to the company's pits at Market Overton. All were fitted with electric headlamps and were amongst the last steam engines to work the ironfields.

Stewarts & Lloyds purchased their final steam engine in 1958 and *Achilles* was one of the last two to be delivered. The class was finally replaced by diesels in 1969.

Some preserved examples are listed under 'Preserved Ironstone Locomotives' on page 179.

Manning Wardle/Kitson/Robert Stephenson   Pl. 113, 115–6, 118–9
and Hawthorn 0–6–0STs

Manning Wardle & Co. Ltd., Boyne Engine Works, Hunslet, Leeds

Manning Wardle & Co. of Leeds commenced operations in 1858 and were well regarded for their distinctive steam locomotive designs. A perfect example is shown in these splendid tanks, the first of which was built in 1910. They were a 16″ cylinder design, that had a long and varied history and became noted for their working on Stewarts & Lloyds Mineral system, Staffordshire Collieries, Munitions factories and even Austin Motor Works at Longbridge. They have furthermore been used as contractor's engines.

Visitors to Pen Green at Corby were often confused by the same design having been built by various companies and the reason for this occurrance was the popularity of the design over a long period of years.

The original locomotives were built by Manning Wardle and in 1927 when that company closed, Kitson took over the goodwill and perpetuated the design to order. In passing it may be mentioned that Kitson are noted for having built many main line locomotives including 5 of the London, Brighton and South Coast Atlantics.

In 1938 Kitsons closed and Robert Stephenson & Hawthorn acquired their drawings and built, at the request of Stewarts & Lloyds, further locomotives to the original Manning design in 1940/41.

Preserved examples are listed on page 179.

Avonside 0–6–0ST   Pl. 114
Avonside Engine Co. Ltd., Bristol

In 1841 Stothert Slaughter of Avonside Works, Bristol, was formed, a
company that became responsible for the building of many early Great
Western Railway locomotives. By 1864 this organisation had become the
well known Avonside Engine Co. and they continued to feature promi-
nently in private locomotive construction until closure in 1934, after
which the Hunslet Company took over their goodwill and manufacturing
rights.

The locomotive illustrated was a standard Avonside design of Class B5,
the first of which was built for the Buxton Lime Firms Co. (now part of
ICI) in 1921. Some 30 engines of this type were built over the following 10
years. A few dimensional differences occurred within the class. The
cylinder diameter varied between $14\frac{1}{2}''$ and $15''$ and the driving wheel
diameter between $3'\,3''$ and $3'\,6''$.

Over the years the type has occurred in collieries, steel works, water
works and upon ironstone systems. At the beginning of 1970 some
survivors were still at work including 3 at Snowdown Colliery in Kent and
others on the Yorkshire Coalfields.

A preserved example may be found on the Bluebell Railway in Sussex.

Hawthorn Leslie 0–6–0ST   Pl. 117

This pleasing design dates back prior to 1920 and was continued after
Hawthorn Leslie merged with Robert Stephenson. In addition to their
being chosen as the standard engine for Stewart & Lloyds Steel Works at
Corby other examples appeared at collieries in north-east England and
various docks. The majority of the ones at Corby were converted to burn
oil fuel and in 1970 9 still remained in use.

One of the withdrawn engines from Corby has been acquired for
private preservation as listed on page 179.

Andrew Barclay 0–4–0ST   Pl. 118–20, 125
Andrew Barclay Sons & Co. Ltd., Caledonia Works, Kilmarnock, Scotland

This company were well known locomotive builders from the 1860s
through to the mid 1950s. Although many of their designs may still be
found at work, Andrew Barclay have completely finished dealing with
steam engines and are now totally engaged in the construction and
overhaul of diesels.

The company produced a long line of 0–4–0STs and 0–6–0STs basically
to the same design and simply enlarged them as the years passed.
Understandably, many of their products went to Scottish industrial
establishments, especially collieries, steel works and gasworks.

Similar locomotives to the one illustrated worked at Stewarts & Lloyds
of Newport, Monmouthshire, and others in English power stations,
gasworks, chemical works, potteries, cement works and ironstone mines.
The subject of the picture is a typical Andrew Barclay design and was built
in 1940. This engine was broken up at Cohens of Kettering in 1969 but
similar ones of a strong family resemblance may be found in preserved
form at Quainton Road Railway Society, Bucks, the Keighley and Worth
Valley Railway, and the Scottish Railway Preservation Society, Falkirk.

Hunslet 16″ 0–6–0ST
Pl. 121–4, 126–7

Here is one of the most successful and characteristic industrial loco-motives ever built. It is Hunslet's 16″ saddle tank design of 1923 which was one of the immediate forerunners of the well known Hunslet Austerity locomotives of 1943. Despite being somewhat superseded by the larger Austerity design these 16″ engines were still being built in the late 1950s and very large numbers have been constructed. Some have been fitted with the Hunslet Special Blast Pipe.

Always a familiar type amongst industrial systems, they worked at such places as collieries – especially in the Leeds area – ironstone concerns and power stations; of the latter, the ones at Uskmouth and Ferrybridge are typical examples. Furthermore the type was chosen by such companies as Guest Keen and Baldwins of Cardiff and the Austin Motor Works at Longbridge.

The class has rather subtle lines that vividly recall locomotives of a much older design and consequently are splendid to observe in action. Many still remain at work and it is expected that they will be amongst the last of the steam designs to disappear from the industrial scene.

Further reference may be found during the discussion on their larger relations the Austerities. See page 137.

Bagnall 0–6–0ST
Pl. 128

The remarkable point about these locomotives is that out of the 7 built no less than 4 have been preserved. This is especially fortunate as without doubt they are one of the loveliest modern saddle tanks ever built.

The Glascote Colliery near Tamworth purchased the first of these 15″ engines in 1934 and the other 6 were built to the order of the Ministry of Supply in 1941/2 for work in the Staveley Mineral ironstone pits. As the illustration shows one of these was still at work at their Cranford pit in 1969.

It is unfortunate that no further examples were constructed by Bagnall and one assumes that the reason for this was their later involvement in the building of the Hunslet Austerities.

Some preserved examples are listed on page 179.

Ex-Etat 0–4–0TA
Pl. 130

The locomotive illustrated constitutes one of the last survivors of a standard Etat shunting type built between 1914 and 1922. Originally the class numbered 144 engines.

The design is of 2 cylinders with 19″ × 23½″ proportion, a boiler pressure of 170 lb per sq in. and driving wheels of 4′ 3″ diameter. Total weight is 64 tons and length 36′. These locomotives have a vintage air about them and they are further characterised by the sloping tanks which give an improved view for the footplate men.

In 1970 a few survivors remained at work in the Le Mans and Nantes area.

Ex-L.M.S. 4MT 2–6–0 3000 Class
Pl. 131

When H. G. Ivatt succeeded Fairburn as C.M.E. of the L.M.S. in 1945 there was a need for some small general purpose locomotives to replace many of the older pre-grouping types that were still in existence. Stanier had fully provided for the system's larger engine requirements but he had produced few designs for lighter duties. As part of Ivatt's remedy, he introduced the 3000 Class, the first three of which were built by the L.M.S. in December 1947 and the remainder by British Railways.

They were a radical design and quite a departure from previous L.M.S. practice. In the 3000s we see the beginnings of some characteristics used in the later B.R. Standards, a high pitched boiler and running plate, regulator rod situated on the outside of the engine and rocking grates. Another very modern innovation was the fitting of tender-cabs which enabled them to run satisfactorily in either direction. These were especially suitable for cross country work. In addition some were specially fitted with tablet pick-ups for single line operation. This design formed the basis for the B.R. 76000s. The first 30 engines were fitted with double chimneys but these were found to be ineffective and were later removed.

No less than 162 were built and became very widely spread over the ex-L.M.S. system. Other engines of the type went to the Eastern Region to operate passenger trains in the Peterborough and Kings Lynn area and to the North Eastern Region for working local freight.

Scrapping of the class began in 1963 but some remained to be amongst the last of B.R.s steam locomotives. The last few worked from Lostock Hall depot in 1968 and when these were withdrawn one was despatched to the Severn Valley Railway at Bridgnorth for preservation.

Ex-L.M.S. 4MT 2–6–4T   Pl. 132

The locomotive depicted was one of the last survivors from a Stanier design of 1935. After slight variations the type was continued by Fairburn and over 450 examples had been built by 1951. It is likely that this number would have risen much higher had it not been for B.R. further developing the design and thus creating the Standard 4MT 80000 Class of 1951. The L.M.S. found them ideal for suburban and inter-city passenger trains and their adequate dimensions rendered them suitable for even the heaviest of these duties. Their acceleration was rapid and speeds well in the 70s were often recorded.

Leading dimensions were 2 cylinders $19\frac{1}{2}'' \times 26''$, a 200 lb per sq in. boiler pressure and driving wheels of 5′ 9″ diameter.

They were found working around all the principal cities served by the L.M.S. in both the Midlands and the North and furthermore were extensively used in the Glasgow area. After nationalisation some large batches were drafted onto the Southern Region.

The first ones were withdrawn in 1961 and the remainder suffered a rapid demise as they became redundant through electrification and dieselisation. Amongst the last duties they undertook was the banking of trains over Beattock and miscellaneous shunting and station pilot work. Unfortunately the Stanier series are now extinct but preserved examples of the almost identical Fairburn type are listed on page 162.

Ex-L.N.E.R. B1 Class 4–6–0   Pl. 135

The B1s were an L.N.E.R. standard wartime design by Edward Thompson and they became that railway's counterpart of the L.M.S.

Stanier 5MT 4–6–0s. The first one emerged from Darlington Works in 1942 and the original series was named after African animals causing them to be known as the Antelope Class. They sported such fine names as *Impala, Oryx, Blackbuck, Klipspringer* and *Roedeer*. A total of 410 engines were built, many of the later ones coming from the North British Works at Glasgow. Building continued after nationalisation.

Essentially the class was a utility design produced in a time of need and it was due to these circumstances that they were built to have identical parts to other leading L.N.E.R. classes. Accordingly the boiler and firebox were the same as Gresley's Sandringham 4–6–0s, the cylinders were of the Gresley K2 2–6–0s and wheels of the V2 2–6–2s. The B1s dimensions included 2 cylinders of 20″ × 26″, 225 lb per sq in. boiler pressure and 6′ 2″ diameter driving wheels.

As with their L.M.S. counterparts, the advent of such a large class of mixed traffic engines inevitably meant the withdrawal of some older engines and the B1s did much to seal the fate of such classes as the G.N., G.C. and N.E. Atlantics along with the G.C. and N.E. 4–6–0s. In addition many fine old 4–4–0s passed into history. The class performed excellent work over the whole of the L.N.E.R. systems and put up some sparkling performances during the locomotive exchanges in 1948.

Scrapping commenced in the early 1960s and by 1968 the last survivors had been withdrawn. A preserved example is listed on page 162.

Ex-W.D. Austerity 2–8–0   Pl. 138

When war broke out in 1939 it was thought that operations might take on a similar aspect to those of the first world war and that a large number of locomotives would be required for duties overseas. Accordingly, R.A. Riddles – who was later responsible for the B.R. Standards – prepared a special emergency design of 2–8–0s for the Ministry of Supply. Some of Stanier's L.M.S. 2–8–0s had already been commissioned by the Ministry and the new design was based upon this class, with which it was to have a wide interchangeability of parts.

The new 2–8–0 Austerities were built by the North British Works in Glasgow and the Vulcan Foundry in Lancashire, almost 1,000 being constructed between 1943–45. Outwardly they bore little resemblence to the Stanier 8Fs for they looked the epitomy of an austere wartime engine and immediately became hailed by the locomotive fraternities as the ugliest creatures ever to take to the rails.

They did service in many countries including France, Belgium and Egypt and as the Allies drove the enemy out of the occupied countries so the Austerities became increasingly relied upon for vital supplies. When the war was over most of them returned to Britain. In 1947 the L.N.E.R. purchased 200 and later on B.R. acquired 500 and thus they became one of the important freight classes.

The leading dimensions were 2 cylinders of 19″ × 28″, boiler pressure 225 lb per sq in., driving wheels 4′ 8½″ diameter. Their coal and water capacities were 9 tons and 5,000 gallons respectively.

Although possessing a rather weird ugliness they were not without character and for many years were an important part of the railway scene in Yorkshire and N.E. England being extensively employed on the heavy coal trains. Some 60 of them were allocated to Wakefield. In addition the type was frequently seen on the ex-Midland Railway main line operating coal and iron ore traffic between Wellingborough and the North.

Despite being a 'stop gap' design their excellence in performance ensured them a long life and it was not until steam was eliminated in N.E. England that the final ones disappeared. One notable feature was the poor balancing of the driving wheels which caused them to oscillate and the resulting 'clank' of the motion earned them the nickname of 'Aussie-plonks'. One of the class was named *Vulcan* in commemoration of its origin.

Numerous as the class was the preservation movement ignored them which resulted in their extinction and now in retrospect they are to me a very serious ommission in the British preservation lists. Fortunately a similar locomotive does exist today in the form of a sister 2–10–0 of the same period. This engine, named *Gordon,* is preserved at the premises of the Longmoor Military Railway in Hampshire.

Ex-N.E.R. Q6 0–8–0   Rear endpaper

This scene, from West Hartlepool in 1965, depicts two of the memorable Q6 0–8–0s that characterised N.E. England for many years. Designed by Sir Vincent Raven, C.M.E. of the North Eastern Railway, the first locomotive appeared in 1913 and the class eventually totalled 120 engines, all of which had been built by 1921.

The North Eastern Railway was noted for its high density of freight traffic and these engines provided a valuable source of power, especially on the long and heavy coal trains from the Northumberland and Durham coalfields.

Leading dimensions were: 2 cylinders $20'' \times 26''$, boiler pressure 180 lb per sq in, driving wheels $4' 7\frac{1}{2}''$; the total weight was 110 tons. The Q6s were amongst the very last vintage steam locomotives to remain in service on British Rail, for although scrapping of the class commenced in 1960 some survived until the cessation of steam power in N.E. England in 1967.

Their survival inevitably attracted a considerable influx of enthusiasts, for the Q6s were regarded as a valuable fragment of our industrial past. It was this industrial past that had created – with a vividity seldom equalled elsewhere – the huge industrial complex of N.E. England, an awe-inspiring area of grime-stained towns and grey slate roofs set against a backcloth of collieries, steelworks and factory chimneys. Such was the famous North East and this was the world to which the Q6s intrinsically belonged.

Fortunately, due to the enterprise of the North Eastern Locomotive Preservation Group, one Q6 – No. 63395 – has been saved from the scrap heap and it is hoped that this locomotive will operate on the North Yorkshire Moors Preservation Society's line between Grosmont and Pickering.

A similar locomotive is at present stored in the B.R. national relics collection at Brighton. This is a Q7 0–8–0, a larger 3-cylinder version of the Q6, of which 15 were built by the N.E.R. between 1919 and 1924. They became extinct in 1962. Unlike the Q6, however, this engine – No. 63460 – is not expected to work again.

THE RAILWAY PRESERVATION MOVEMENT

The Railway Preservation Movement in Britain

Not many years ago the steam locomotive was, from a working point of view, doomed to extinction and once the proposals of the 1955 modernisation programme began to take effect it became abundantly clear that this extinction would occur during the 1960s. Class after class of Britain's locomotive heritage was being ruthlessly cast onto the scrap heap and although a limited collection of locomotives was destined for placing in various museums it would constitute an impoverished substitute for all that was to be lost.

Fortunately in the eleventh hour there emerged some far-sighted and enterprising groups of enthusiasts who were not to be satisfied with the inanimate museums of the governmental establishments. They maintained that the steam locomotive must be retained in all its working glory that future generations might see it in a true perspective.

The dedication and unselfishness of these early pioneers enabled events to turn the complete circle, for as the nationalised railway dispensed with steam power so newly formed preservation companies restored it. Once again it became possible to buy shares in a railway, to travel by private and individualistic lines and even to be employed by a private railway enterprise. History was beginning to repeat itself.

The opposition that the preservationists encountered may be compared to that which faced the original companies some 130 years earlier and serious objections invariably had to be faced from such bodies as the Ministry of Transport, Town and Country Planning, Development Organisations and country lovers.

It may clearly be seen then that once a particular stretch of railway had been closed there could be many reasons why it should remain that way and in such circumstances a group of people who wished to restore the railway with steam locomotives clearly constituted a nigger in the woodpile.

In addition to such opposition was the huge financial involvement necessary to enable even the most modest of dreams to be fulfilled. The purchase, transportation and restoration of a derelict locomotive or item of rolling stock was costly enough but when whole sections of railway came to be bought then it was clearly a job for professionals.

The basic essentials involved were the purchase of land and track, along with stations and buildings on the route. On completion, a suitable selection of locomotives and rolling stock had to be transferred to the site and restoration work begun in earnest. Invariably the whole concern would be in a run-down and depleted condition and gangs of voluntary enthusiasts faced years of toil. Track and rolling stock had to be brought up to Ministry of Transport standards whilst locomotives had to undergo boiler tests to meet insurance stipulations.

With thousands of pounds poured out on such requirements the companies' legal administrations had to meet and negotiate with all opposition before application for a light railway order without which no public services could commence.

The labour and finances have principally been provided by the nation's enthusiasts. It was fortunate that the steam locomotive had always attracted a complete cross-section of society and it was this that went a long way towards saving it, for amongst its devotees were many business and professional people who were prepared to donate or loan large sums of money. Further finances came from society memberships, special rail tours, shares and numerous collections and appeals.

The nation's enthusiasts rallied round once the incentive had been provided for a project and the one thing that enabled them to gain ground against such terrific odds was that it was 'now or never'; the railways as they knew and loved them were being ruthlessly destroyed – they had to succeed and quickly.

In almost every case the perpetuation of steam was the motivation and some companies never thought further than this, although others set out to achieve a profitable return upon their investments as quickly as possible. All, however, were convinced – as were the early railway pioneers of the 1820s – that both they, the community at large and generations of the future would benefit by their actions.

A further parallel with railway history was seen in the piecemeal way in which the preservation was conducted, and as the movement progressed companies derived from local interests began to compete for support. It soon became apparent that the majority of schemes held some emotional appeal to every railway lover and it became the policy for many people to contribute a little money to each. Here one was reminded of the financial crash of the late 1840s which was partly caused by a somewhat over-ambitious building of railways and warnings came from responsible individuals throughout the world of railway interest that unless some form of control be exercised and a national plan envisaged the movement must irretrievably suffocate itself.

The result of this was the formation in 1958 of the Association of Railway Preservation Societies which was designed – much in the way that the Clearing House of 1841 was intended – to protect the interests of the movement generally. Under its cohesive influence much progress was made and it provided a common meeting ground for groups with similar aims, assistance with legal problems and a platform for negotiations with British Railways. In short it added more professionalism to the whole movement and, under the chairmanship of Captain Peter Manisty R.N., has furthermore made several bulk purchases of locomotives on behalf of different companies and assisted in the placing of many important relics. By 1967 they represented 25 separate concerns and in 1970 covered 90% of the voluntary effort in Great Britain.

Despite the efforts of the Association some conflicting issues continued to occur. This was an emotional and passionate business and a few groups who saw a possibility for success refused to abandon their ideals to support a similar yet entirely different project on the opposite side of the country.

Support continued to pour in and the enthusiasts' resources were fully extended. These were the final years of steam on British Railways and rail tours, travel, photographic and recording expenses had to be met in order to enjoy what was left. Notwithstanding such deviations the companies continued to blazon their impassioned demands with such themes as 'Do you want to see all the 8Fs go to the scrapyard?' 'Steam tomorrow—with your help' '1969 and you?' 'The W. and L. invites you . . . ' 'Invest now in . . . '.

Inevitably the locomotives acquired were in excess of the quantity needed to operate the route mileage that had been restored. This was not regarded as a particular problem as it was the intention of many owners to operate them over British Railways metals with special trains. However B.R. announced that upon the cessation of normal steam working in August 1968 no further steam locomotives would be allowed on the system. One argument put forward was that once the motive power modernisations had been completed steam would not be allowed to impair the modern image.

B.R. remained adamant over this matter and the question arose of what was to become of the larger engines upon which thousands of pounds had been spent in restoration and overhauls. Owing to weight restrictions the branch lines owned by the various companies were unsuitable, quite apart from which a giant express engine could not be put through its paces on a secondary line of only a few miles in length.

This led to an obvious answer; the narrow gauge had successfully been saved, so had the rural country branches, and now main line companies were needed. The Beeching Plan provided the ideal material for such concerns as an increasing number of main line stretches were being abandoned by British Railways. The possibilities were unlimited and the argument behind so many schemes was simply 'If B.R. cannot operate profitably with diesels then we can with steam'.

Such has been the wonderful and worthwhile effort during the 1950s and '60s by a country with an estimated 2 million railway enthusiasts (some 4% of the population). All that had been needed was for some enlightened spirits to show the way by working as united teams exercising firm management and control and a huge movement developed to support them.

By 1970 a grand total of some 100 route miles of preserved steam railway were in operation in addition to which a further 60 miles was in the process of negotiation by various established concerns. Given the dedication and fortunes that the last two decades have brought the mid-'70s may see the operative figure exceed 150 miles.

The total number of locomotives preserved throughout Britain is in excess of 700 – an equivalent $3\frac{1}{2}$% of the total B.R. steam stock of 1948! Certainly a lot of these are from narrow gauge or industrial concerns but these are none the less fascinating and have greatly contributed to the diversity of origins and backgrounds.

It is impossible to estimate how many further locomotives will be saved as they are still being acquired from the National Coal Board and other industrial concerns and from the huge stocks of ex-B.R. engines dumped at Barry. In addition to this, one company has commenced importing locomotives from abroad and it is possible that the next decade will see the total rise to 1,000. Already the last 20 years has averaged out with one locomotive being preserved per two weeks!

To the layman the steam age has passed, to children in schools it is part of their history lessons, but just beneath the surface lies a world of splendour that rivals pre-grouping days and belongs as much to the present as do the latest diesel and electric types of British Rail.

Our sociologists tell us the future is to be one of 'means and leisure' and in an ever streamlining world these little havens of history will surely prove their right to a place. As the opportunities for tourism continue so will more and more people be able to enjoy the uniqueness of a steam-worked railway the foundations of which were laid by those dedicated pioneers of the 1950s.

The Historical Outline

The 'Pen-y-daren' of the preservation world occurred in 1927 when the Stephenson Locomotive Society purchased *Gladstone,* one of Stroudley's famous 0-4-2 express locomotives, from the Southern Railway. Several engines had been preserved prior to this date by various companies but this was the first private action by enthusiasts. The engine was eventually placed in York Museum where it still resides.

Many years were to elapse, however, before the first railway was acquired by a preservation group, but after the second world war concern was mounting over the disappearance of the Welsh narrow gauge lines. These were unique little railways that had been constructed during the industrial revolution for conveying slate from the quarries high in the mountains and all of them were approaching the end of their days. Under the initiative of L.T.C. Rolt, a leading writer upon transport affairs, a meeting was called in Birmingham on 11 October 1950 with a view to saving the Talyllyn Railway, which at that time was in a rundown condition and due to close. A society was successfully formed which eventually took over the railway and, ignoring the numerous critics who maintained that a railway could not be run by enthusiasts, proceeded to renovate it. Years of struggle culminated in success and passenger traffic increased year by year until a restored railway existed that drew tourists not only from many parts of Britain but also the world. As an additional attraction a Narrow Gauge Museum has been built alongside Towyn Wharf Station.

At a time when preservation was in its infancy this success inspired others and thoughts became centred on the derelict Festiniog Railway that lay some 30 miles to the north at Portmadoc. It had been closed in 1946 and had the distinction of being the oldest public narrow gauge railway in the world, having been opened in 1836. Here was a potential railway paradise situated in an excellent tourist area and within a year of the Talyllyn movement being formed the Festiniog Railway Society came into being. In 1954 control of the line was aquired by Mr Alan Pegler, of later *Flying Scotsman* fame, and supported by the Society the first train ran again in July 1955 after terrific legal, financial, and practical difficulties had been overcome. Just 10 years later the summer service carried 150,000 passengers and new records continued to be broken over succeeding years – resulting in a figure of 319,500 in 1969.

Before the 1950s had passed plans had been made to reopen a section of the 'Bluebell' line, so named after the abundance of spring flowers in the area, which originally ran as part of the L.B.S.C.R. from Culver Junction to Horsted Keynes. The line was closed in 1958 and its successful reopening signified the first of many subsequent negotiations with British Railways for the purchase of standard gauge routes. In 1959 three students formed the Bluebell Preservation Society and after a successful bid to prevent a scrap contractor from lifting the metals a lease was obtained and by August 1960 the first services had commenced. This was to become a magnificent working museum in the heart of rural Sussex.

With one standard gauge line in operation the main stream of events turned again upon Wales where a passenger and agricultural line which had been opened in 1903 to operate between Welshpool and Llanfair Caereinion in Montgomeryshire was due to be closed by British Railways. A society had been formed to save the line prior to its closure in 1956 but it was not until 1960 that a company was created which after obtaining a lease and light railway order commenced passenger services in 1963 over a section of the route. A tragedy occurred the following year when the bridge over the River Banwy was damaged by floods. This was a serious setback but fortunately a detachment of Royal Engineers repaired the damage and service was resumed as normal in 1966. This railway, though not strictly in a tourist area, is situated alongside a main holiday route which carries heavy tourist traffic into central Wales and many a family 'not in the know' has been astounded to find this delightful steam stronghold. The company eventually hope to reach the outskirts of Welshpool.

Another mining railway was saved in the early 1960s in the form of the miniature 1' 3" Ravenglass and Eskdale which had, since its construction in 1873, carried iron ore, granite and passengers. It originally connected the ironstone mines at Boot with the Furness Railway at Ravenglass. The passenger service was discontinued on the R. and E. as it was upon many other narrow gauge lines during the 1930s. It was reinstated in 1945 but the later closure of the granite quarries in 1953 led to the railway's impending closure. It was saved by an amateur preservation group and the company was set on its feet by money granted from a Birmingham stockbroker. The 7-mile route later became an immense attraction and despite the somewhat small size of its locomotives it has become a firm institution amongst Britain's preserved railways.

The successful restoration of the Bluebell line created a precedent that was to hasten the preservation movement on its way by arousing the interest of the business world. British Railways were regularly dispensing with branch lines, many of which it appeared could be acquired and converted to run at a profit.

On 29 September 1962 the Western News mentioned that 14 professional and business men intended to reopen the ex-G.W. branch line from Totnes to Ashburton which had closed earlier that year. This was a departure from the purely enthusiast efforts as it was intended to be a strict business venture and be commercially viable from the earliest possible date. They felt that a working steam service combined with a museum and facilities for souvenirs and refreshments would be highly successful in such a heavy tourist area as Devon.

Their intentions were readily supported by the Great Western Society who already had a collection of locomotives and rolling stock and were only too anxious for an opportunity to restore in working condition some of the former glory of that railway, and what better way to do it than on an ex-G.W. branch line in the heart of Devon. After a long wait due to financial problems the line was finally reopened on 21 May 1969 by no other than Lord Beeching, and so was born one of the most beautiful preserved lines in the world. In Britain it remains unique in that it is devoted to the perpetuation of one particular company, namely the former Great Western Railway. The locomotives and rolling stock all originated from that company (Plate nos. 55 & 56.)

The mid 1960s were the Beeching years, the period when Britain's steam locomotives were fast becoming decimated, and once it became apparent that genuine working lines were an ever increasing possibility, groups of enthusiasts and companies began to purchase locomotives. Some were purchased with the intention of their being used on enthusiasts' specials on British Railways, some with a view to being placed upon one of the preserved lines and others simply to make up collections of engines that could occasionally be steamed, and stored in rented sidings. Undoubtedly the most famous of the locomotive purchases was that made in January 1963 by Mr Alan Pegler of *Flying Scotsman* – originally one of Gresley's A1 Pacifics of 1923. After purchase the locomotive was restored to its appearance of pre-war days and it proceeded to operate enthusiasts' specials all over Britain. It became the most flamboyant advertisement for steam preservation imaginable and was the subject of immense publicity. On its many travels with special trains it brought thousands of people flocking to the stations and linesides of its passage. *Flying Scotsman* was the first of quite a number of express locomotives that have subsequently been purchased and overhauled to main line order. So popular has *Flying Scotsman* proved that in 1969 it left for America with a special train on a 'boost British exports' campaign – and what better advertisement could Britain have used?

On 15 May 1962 a meeting was called in Keighley Temperance Hall by a Mr G.R. Cryer, a local railway enthusiast, who was determined to save the one-time M.R. branch line that ran from Keighley through the Worth Valley and up to Oxenhope. The line was already due for closure by British Railways and at the very first meeting a committee was formed with Mr Cryer as chairman to lead a new and great movement named 'The Keighley and Worth Valley Preservation Society'.

After the branch had closed in June 1962 the Society commenced restoration work; a collection of locomotives and rolling stock began to arrive at Haworth Station which was rented as a headquarters, and many visitors were attracted to the line long before it was reopened. In 1966 a company was formed and the following year saw the agreement signed for purchase of the line. The opening which came on 29 June 1968 was an important advancement for steam lovers all over the country, for the following August was to bring the complete cessation of steam activities on British Rail. The line has thrived ever since and the $4\frac{3}{4}$-mile route contains a gradient of 1 in 58 over which some very full-blooded action can be enjoyed. In addition to its frequent services the line also has an excellent collection of locomotives.

Whilst the final negotiations were being completed for the opening of the Keighley and Worth Valley Railway a fine achievement occurred in the Isle of Man when their 3' 0" gauge system was reinstated.

For economic reasons the Isle of Man Railway Company had been forced to close in 1966 after almost a century of operation and it appeared that this uniquely picturesque system was destined to be committed to the annals of railway history.

After great efforts by the Marquess of Ailsa the reopening was achieved on 3 June 1967 and subsequent support by the Isle of Man tourist board and the Manx Government has enabled the railway to be restored to its former glory.

The reopening was a highly ceremonious occasion: brass bands played, crowds gathered at the lineside and many well known personalities were present. On the footplate of the first train was the Rev. Teddy Boston, owner of the Cadeby Light Railway, at Market Bosworth.

The system is principally operated by 2-4-0Ts of Beyer Peacock design which date back to 1873 and their vintage lineage and resplendent condition vividly recalls the atmosphere of Britain's pre-grouping railways.

Less than two years were to pass before another standard gauge line appeared. This was the Severn Valley Railway Company who succeeded in commencing operations over the ex-G.W. line between Bridgnorth and Hampton Loade. This, like so many others, has been achieved after many years of struggle to obtain its Light Railway Order which British Rail obtained for them on 4 December 1969. It is hoped that this line will eventually be extended and although not operating in a strictly tourist area it is within easy reach of densely populated areas.

Although the operating lines represented the ultimate hopes of the preservationists, many of the locomotive collections have nevertheless proved immensely popular especially when regular steam days are featured. Noteworthy among these is the Standard Gauge Steam Trust at Tyseley in Birmingham pioneered by Mr Patrick Whitehouse who has also played a large part in the original Welsh narrow gauge projects and the Dart Valley. Largely through his efforts, Tyseley has become a great steam centre for the Midlands and now upon the site of the old G.W. depot are housed several main line engines in first class running order. Additional loco-motives and extensions are envisaged for the future. (Plate nos. 1, 8 and 9.)

In such a precarious movement as railway preservation it is inevitable that some worthwhile schemes must either fall by the wayside or become seriously held up. Two of the finest collections of locomotives in the country are intended to form the basis of working lines. These are the Kent and East Sussex, who are based at Rolvenden and after many years are still negotiating for authorisation to operate services between Robertsbridge and Tenterden, and the Lakeside Railway who have an excellent stud of locomotives at the ex-B.R. steam sheds at Carnforth. The Lakeside came into being to operate between Ulverston and Lakeside (Windermere) in the heart of a tourist area but due to many operational problems are still confined to their depot base. Both companies hope for a brighter future which will enable them to operate fully but meanwhile they put on steaming days and attract many hundreds of visitors.

Many new and exciting schemes are in the embryo stage and despite the incredible progress that has been made the movement is still in its infancy. The size and numbers of workable locomotives available have for several years demanded a stretch of main line instead of the traditional branches.

One proposal to meet the demand for a main line stretch is in hand by the Main Line Preservation Group who intend to purchase a section of the old Great Central main line between Leicester and Ruddington in Nottinghamshire. This line, built as late as the turn of the century and closed on 5 May 1969, was designed for the bigger and faster trains of that period and as such would be capable of taking the largest of the preserved engines. The intention is to operate a twin-track system to enable normal running at realistic speeds, and in view of the tourist, educational and recreational attractions the company hopes to become a charitable trust. Headquarters are at Loughborough Central Station which has already been extensively renovated by volunteers.

Amongst the many new secondary lines envisaged is the North Norfolk Railway Co., intending to run from Sheringham to Weybourne with eventual extensions to Holt. To the north lies the North Yorkshire Moors Railway Preservation Society who have signed a contract to purchase from British Rail the track from Grosmont to Ellersbeck and the track bed onwards to Pickering. When this line becomes operative their locomotive stock will be increased by additions presented by the North Eastern Locomotive Preservation Group.

Additions to the Welsh Narrow Gauge Railways are hoped for with the Welsh Highland Railway and the Llanberis Lake section of the old Padarn Railway. Again, all these are situated in established tourist areas.

As British Rail further reduces its system, the hopes and aspirations of the preservationists will continue to flourish, but even in the eventuality of no further successes, Britain has already a truly fascinating collection of steam railways all of which appear to have a wonderful future ahead of them.

I PRINCIPAL RAILWAYS OPERATING STEAM PASSENGER SERVICES

(Full details of operations along with timetables may be obtained upon application to the line concerned)

Standard Gauge		Route	Mileage
Bluebell Railway		Sheffield Park – Horsted Keynes	5
Keighley and Worth Valley Railway		Keighley – Oxenhope	$4\frac{3}{4}$
Dart Valley Railway		Totnes – Buckfastleigh	7
Severn Valley Railway		Bridgnorth – Hampton Loade	$4\frac{1}{2}$

Narrow Gauge	Gauge	Route	Mileage
Festiniog Railway	1' 11$\frac{5}{8}$"	Portmadoc (Harbour) – Dduallt	$9\frac{3}{4}$
Talyllyn Railway	2' 3"	Towyn – Abergynolwyn	$6\frac{3}{4}$
Welshpool and Llanfair	2' 6"	Llanfair Caereinion – Castle Caereinion	$4\frac{1}{4}$
Ravenglass and Eskdale	1' 3"	Ravenglass – Dalegarth	7
Lincolnshire Coast Light Railway	2' 0"	Humberston (North Sea Lane)– Humberston (South Sea Lane)	1
Isle of Man Steam Railway Co.	3' 0"	Douglas – Port Erin	$16\frac{1}{2}$
Sittingbourne and Kemsley Light Railway	2'6"	Sittingbourne – Kemsley	2

The following three concerns, although not actually constituting a part of the preservation movement, are nevertheless steam-operated lines reliant upon tourist trade, and as such are of excellent interest.

The Vale of Rheidol is operated by British Rail although a supporters' association has been formed. The Snowdon is Britain's only 'mountain railway' whilst the Romney Hythe and Dymchurch Railway has been privately operated as a passenger line since 1927.

Railway	Gauge	Route	Mileage
Vale of Rheidol	1' 11$\frac{1}{2}$"	Aberystwyth – Devils Bridge	$11\frac{1}{4}$
Snowdon Mountain Railway	2' 7$\frac{1}{2}$"	Llanberis – Snowdon Summit	5
Romney Hythe and Dymchurch	1' 3"	Hythe – Dungeness	$13\frac{3}{4}$

II ORGANISATIONS AND SOCIETIES POSSESSING COLLECTIONS OF LOCOMOTIVES

(The majority of the undermentioned groups have special 'steam days' and feature a limited amount of siding trips)

Kent and East Sussex Railway	*	Rolvenden
Standard Gauge Steam Trust	*	Tyseley
Lakeside Railway	*	Carnforth
Bressingham Hall	*	Diss, Norfolk
Great Western Society	*	Didcot

London Railway Preservation Society *	Quainton Road, Bucks.
Dinting Railway Centre	Dinting, Derbyshire
Dowty Preservation Centre	Ashchurch, Glos.
South Eastern Steam Centre	Ashford
Scottish Railway Preservation Society	Falkirk
Helical Springs Limited	Lytham Creek, Lancashire
Railway Preservation Society	Chasewater
North Yorkshire Moors Preservation Society	Goathland Station, Yorkshire
North Norfolk Railway Company	Sheringham

(The following have increased running facilities and passenger trips are operated from time to time)

Lochty Branch Railway	East Fife
Foxfield Light Railway	Blythe Bridge, Staffs.
Leighton Buzzard Light Railway	Leighton Buzzard
Bulmers Cider Company	Hereford
Middleton Railway Trust	Leeds

* Especially recommended

III SOME PRINCIPAL MUSEUMS HOLDING LOCOMOTIVES AS STATIC EXHIBITS

Clapham Transport Museum   *
Science Museum, South Kensington   *
York Railway Museum   *
Great Western Museum, Swindon   *
Leicester Museum of Technology   *
Penrhyn Castle Museum, Bangor   *
Birmingham Museum of Science and Industry
Glasgow Transport Museum   *
Royal Scottish Museum, Edinburgh
Narrow Gauge Museum, Towyn   *
Museum of Staffordshire Life, Stafford
Newcastle Science Museum
Bristol Museum
Belfast Transport Museum   *

* Especially recommended

The foregoing schedules have given account of the principal preservation establishments in Great Britain and the majority of the places mentioned have a wide and varied selection of locomotives. In addition are many very small narrow gauge concerns operating steam services as well as the numerous locomotives owned by smaller groups and individuals, and found residing in many places ranging from public houses to back gardens. Noteworthy amongst these are the ex-L.M.S. express passenger types preserved by Butlins at their Pwllheli, Ayr, Minehead and Skegness Camps.

Many further examples are held by British Rail, awaiting restoration and placing.

A SELECTION OF PRESERVED BRITISH RAILWAY LOCOMOTIVES

Locomotive	Type	Date of Design	Designer	Company	General Details	Place of Preservation
WYLAM DILLY	2–2–0	1813	William Hedley	Wylam Colliery	The earliest locomotive in existence	Royal Scottish Museum, Edinburgh
LOCOMOTION No. 1	0–4–0	1825	George Stephenson	Stockton and Darlington	First locomotive to operate on a public railway	Darlington Bank Top Station
ROCKET	0–2–2	1829	George Stephenson	Liverpool and Manchester	Winner of the Rainhill Trials and a milestone in steam locomotive development	Science Museum, London
NORTH STAR	2–2–2	1837	Robert Stephenson and Co.	Great Western	A replica of an early broad gauge 7′ passenger locomotive	Swindon Museum
COLUMBINE	2–2–2	1845	Alexander Allan	Grand Junction (later London and North Western)	Early passenger type	York Museum
DERWENT	0–6–0	1845	Timothy Hackworth	Stockton and Darlington	Excellent example of an early 0–6–0 freight locomotive	Darlington Bank Top Station
COPPERNOB	0–4–0	1846	Edward Bury	Furness	An example of an early Bury locomotive. A similar type (in 2–2–0 form) was the principal power for the London-Birmingham railway	Clapham Museum
CORNWALL	2–2–2	1847	Francis Trevithick	London and North Western	In rebuilt form. Originally the driving axle was placed above the boiler for a low centre of gravity	Clapham Museum
No. 23	4–4–0T	1864	Beyer Peacock Co.	Metropolitan	A fine example of an early tank locomotive fitted with condensers for working the London Underground system	Clapham Museum
156 CLASS No. 158A	2–4–0	1866	Matthew Kirtley	Midland	An early express design to the 2–4–0 wheel arrangement	Leicester Museum of Technology
STIRLING'S No. 1	4–2–2	1870	Patrick Stirling	Great Northern	One of the most graceful designs in British locomotive history	York Museum
BOXHILL Terrier Class	0–6–0T	1872	William Stroudley	London, Brighton and South Coast	Light duty tank engines, 10 of which have been preserved	Clapham Museum

(Other examples may be found on the Bluebell Railway, Sussex, and on the Kent and East Sussex Railway)

Locomotive	Type	Date of Design	Designer	Company	General Details	Place of Preservation
JOHNSON SHUNTING TANK No. 1708	0–6–0T	1874	Samuel Johnson	Midland	A standard MR design for shunting duty	Keighley and Worth Valley Railway
NE No. 910	2–4–0	1875	Edward Fletcher	North Eastern	Express passenger design	York Museum
COAL TANK No. 1054	0–6–2T	1881	Francis Webb	London and North Western	General duty engines used throughout the entire L.N.W.R. system	Penrhyn Castle Museum, Bangor

A SELECTION OF PRESERVED BRITISH RAILWAY LOCOMOTIVES

Locomotive	Type	Date of Design	Designer	Company	General Details	Place of Preservation
GLADSTONE	0–4–2	1882	William Stroudley	London, Brighton and South Coast	An express design of considerable beauty	York Museum
RADIAL TANK No. 488	4–4–2T	1882	William Adams	London and South Western	Well proportioned tank design for general duties	Bluebell Railway, Sussex
DEAN GOODS No. 2516	0–6–0	1883	William Dean	Great Western	Standard design goods engine and used extensively overseas during both world wars	Swindon Museum
No. 123	4–2–2	1886	Dugald Drummond	Caledonian	Another performer in the 1888 railway races to the north and the last single locomotive to remain in service	Glasgow Transport Museum
HARDWICKE Precedent Class	2–4–0	1887	Francis Webb	London and North Western	A standard express type for many years and vividly featured during the races to the north in 1888 and 1895	Clapham Museum
MIDLAND SPINNER, No. 118	4–2–2	1887	Samuel Johnson	Midland	Express locomotive regarded by many as the most gracefully proportioned design to run on any British railway	Leicester Museum of Technology
No. 87	0–6–0T	1890	James Holden	Great Eastern	General purpose freight and suburban passenger locomotive	Clapham Museum
No. 563	4–4–0	1893	William Adams	London and South Western	A beautiful express passenger design of the Victorian era	Clapham Museum
No. 1621	4–4–0	1893	Wilson Worsdell	North Eastern	Another period express passenger design, used in the 1895 races	York Museum
No. 103	4–6–0	1894	David Jones	Highland	The first British 4–6–0 design	Glasgow Transport Museum
No. 419	0–4–4T	1900	John McIntosh	Caledonian	A light passenger design similar to many other 0–4–4Ts of the period	Scottish Railway Preservation Society, Falkirk
No. 1247	0–6–0ST	1897	H. A. Ivatt	Great Northern	Standard shunting tank	Standard Gauge Steam Trust, Tyseley.
HENRY OAKLEY	4–4–2	1898	H. A. Ivatt	Great Northern	First British Atlantic type	York Museum
BIRCH GROVE	0–6–2T	1898	R. Billington	London, Brighton and South Coast	Suburban passenger locomotive	Bluebell Railway, Sussex
JOEM	0–6–0T	1898	Wilson Worsdell	North Eastern	A standard shunting design which enjoyed the distinction of being constructed over many years. This particular example was built by British Railways	Keighley and Worth Valley Railway
D CLASS No. 737	4–4–0	1901	H. Wainwright	South Eastern	Express passenger design of handsome	Clapham Museum

A SELECTION OF PRESERVED BRITISH RAILWAY LOCOMOTIVES

Locomotive	Type	Date of Design	Designer	Company	General Details	Place of Preservation
CITY OF TRURO	4–4–0	1901	William Dean George Churchward	Great Western	Express passenger design and the first locomotive to exceed 100 m.p.h.	Swindon Museum
No. 1000	4–4–0	1902	Samuel Johnson	Midland	This design represents the Midland Railway's compound locomotives. Preserved in the 1914 rebuilt form	Clapham Museum
No. 2818	2–8–0	1903	George Churchward	Great Western	First 2–8–0 heavy freight locomotive to be built in Britain and one of the G.W.R.'s standard designs	Bristol Corporation
LODE STAR Star Class	4–6–0	1906	George Churchward	Great Western	The Star class of express passenger locomotives was an important advancement in G.W.R. locomotive design and the forerunners of the later Castle class	Swindon Museum
4500 CLASS No. 4555	2–6–2T	1906	George Churchward	Great Western	One of the standard tank engine designs for branch lines and cross country work	Dart Valley Railway, Devon
THUNDERSLEY	4–4–2T	1909	Thomas Whitelegg	London, Tilbury and Southend	Passenger tank design for main line working	Bressingham Hall, Diss, Norfolk
No. 102	2–8–0	1911	J. G. Robinson	Great Central	The second important class of 2–8–0 mineral engines to be built and adopted as a standard type by the Railway Operating Department during the first World War	Leicester Museum of Technology
No. 3924	0–6–0	1911	Henry Fowler	Midland	Heavy freight engine later adopted as a standard type by the L.M.S.	Keighley and Worth Valley Railway
(A further locomotive of the later L.M.S. series is scheduled for a place in the Leicester Museum of Technology)						
Q6 CLASS No. 63395	0–8–0	1913	Vincent Raven	North Eastern	Heavy mineral engine for working coal traffic over the North Eastern railway	Intended for use by the North Yorkshire Moors Preservation Group
BUTLER HENDERSON Director Class	4–4–0	1920	J. G. Robinson	Great Central	A distinctive passenger design for main line work	Clapham Museum
GORDON HIGHLANDER	4–4–0	1920	T. E. Heywood	Great North of Scotland	One of the final British 4–4–0 designs and built very much to Victorian styling	Glasgow Transport Museum
G2 CLASS No. 485	0–8–0	1921	H. P. M. Beames	London and North Western	A later development of a long series of 0–8–0 heavy freight locomotives	Leicester Museum of Technology
FLYING SCOTSMAN A3 Class	4–6–2	1922	Sir Nigel Gresley	L.N.E.R.	The first important British Pacific design. They were used for express passenger working over the East Coast route	Doncaster Privately owned

A SELECTION OF PRESERVED BRITISH RAILWAY LOCOMOTIVES

Locomotive	Type	Date of Design	Designer	Company	General Details	Place of Preservation
CAERPHILLY CASTLE Castle Class	4–6–0	1923	C. B. Collett	G.W.R.	A basic express passenger design for 40 years and a direct development of the earlier Star class	Science Museum, Kensington
(Three other examples are preserved: two by G.W.R. Society at Didcot, and the other by Clun Castle Trust, Tyseley, Birmingham)						
47383	0–6–0T	1924	Henry Fowler	L.M.S	A development of an earlier Midland Railway design and adopted as a standard shunting locomotive over the L.M.S. system, commonly termed 'Jintys'.	Severn Valley Railway, Bridgnorth
5600 CLASS No. 6697	0–6–2T	1924	C. B. Collett	G.W.R.	Specially designed for service over the numerous industrial lines of South Wales and intended to replace older designs of the constituent companies in that area	Dowty Preservation Society, Ashchurch
SIR LAMIEL King Arthur Class	4–6–0	1925	R. E. L. Maunsell	S.R.	Development from earlier L.S.W.R. 4–6–0 design and one of the principal express passenger types for the Southern system	Awaiting restoration
2700	2–6–0	1926	George Hughes	L.M.S.	A mixed traffic type for general use	Keighley and Worth Valley Railway
LORD NELSON	4–6–0	1926	R. E. L. Maunsell	S.R.	Heavy express passenger design principally for working continental boat trains between London and Dover	Awaiting restoration
SCOTS GUARDSMAN Royal Scot Class	4–6–0	1927	Henry Fowler	L.M.S.	Express passenger design for 40 years over the west coast route. Preserved as later rebuilt by Stanier	Stockport Locomotive Society, Dinting
(Another example can be seen at Butlins Holiday Camp, Skegness)						
KING GEORGE V King Class	4–6–0	1927	C. B. Collett	G.W.R.	The largest express passenger design on the G.W.R.	Bulmer's Cider Factory, Hereford
BURTON AGNES HALL Hall Class	4–6–0	1928	C. B. Collett	G.W.R.	Standard mixed traffic design developed from earlier Saint class	Great Western Society, Didcot
5700 CLASS No. 3650, 5786	0–6–0PT	1929	C. B. Collett	G.W.R.	Standard class of shunting and light duty engines of which over 850 were built	Bulmer's Cider Company, Hereford.
(The Keighley and Worth Valley Railway also own an example of this class)						
STOWE Schools Class	4–4–0	1930	R. E. L. Maunsell	S.R.	The final and perhaps most successful 4–4–0 design in Britain	Lord Montagu's Museum, Beaulieu, Hants.

(Another locomotive of this type is preserved by British Railways)

A SELECTION OF PRESERVED BRITISH RAILWAY LOCOMOTIVES

Locomotive	Type	Date of Design	Designer	Company	General Details	Place of Preservation
PRINCESS ELIZABETH Princess Royal Class	4–6–2	1933	Sir William Stanier	L.M.S.	The first Pacific design for the L.M.S. for working the heavy expresses over the West Coast Route	Dowty Preservation Society, Ashchurch, Glos.
STANIER BLACK 5	4–6–0	1934	Sir William Stanier	L.M.S.	One of the most successful locomotives ever designed for mixed traffic working, 842 being built between 1934–1950. A total of 12 are preserved	Lakeside Railway Society, Carnforth (6 examples) Keighley and Worth Valley Railway (2 examples)
			(Another example can be found at Butlins Holiday Camp, Pwllheli)			
KOLHAPUR Jubilee Class	4–6–0	1934	Sir William Stanier	L.M.S.	A distinguished express passenger design used throughout the L.M.S. system	Standard Gauge Steam Trust, Tyseley, Birmingham
			(Another example is preserved by The Stockport Locomotive Society)			
8233	2–8–0	1935	Sir William Stanier	L.M.S.	Standard heavy freight design for use throughout the system	Severn Valley Railway, Bridgnorth
MALLARD A4 Class	4–6–2	1935	Sir Nigel Gresley	L.N.E.R.	A streamlined masterpiece in express passenger design and used for the Anglo-Scottish expresses over the East Coast main line. This locomotive holds the world speed record for steam traction of 126 m.p.h.	Clapham Museum
			(Three other examples are preserved privately in Britain)			
GREEN ARROW V2 Class	2–6–2	1936	Sir Nigel Gresley	L.N.E.R.	General purpose mixed traffic locomotive	Leicester Museum of Technology
EARL OF BERKELEY Dukedog Class	4–4–0	1936	C. B. Collett	G.W.R.	A light duty design which enables an excellent idea to be obtained of the G.W. passenger locomotives prior to the Churchward era. They incorporate parts of withdrawn Duke and Bulldog classes	Bluebell Railway, Sussex
CITY OF BIRMINGHAM Princess Coronation Class	4–6–2	1937	Sir William Stanier	L.M.S.	Originally streamlined and used for working Anglo-Scottish expresses over the West Coast Route. Streamlined casing was later removed	Birmingham Museum of Science and Industry
			(Other locomotives of this type can be seen at Butlins Holiday Camps at Minehead and Ayr)			
CLAN LINE Merchant Navy Class	4–6–2	1941	O. V. S. Bulleid	S.R.	An originally streamlined express passenger design for the S.R. Preserved in British Railways rebuilt form	Owned by Merchant Navy Preservation Society, Longmoor, Hants

A SELECTION OF PRESERVED BRITISH RAILWAY LOCOMOTIVES

Locomotive	Type	Date of Design	Designer	Company	General Details	Place of Preservation
B1 CLASS No. 61306	4–6–0	1942	E. Thompson	L.N.E.R.	Standard mixed traffic design	Lakeside Railway Society, Carnforth
GORDON	2–10–0	1943	R. A. Riddles	War Department S.R.	One of a series of Austerity heavy freight locomotives built during World War II	Ministry of Defence, Longmoor, Hants.
BLACKMORE VALE, West Country Class	4–6–2	1945	O. V. S. Bulleid		Lightweight design for express duties throughout the entire S.R. system. Preserved in original air-smoothed condition	Bulleid Preservation Society, Longmoor, Hants.
					(Another locomotive of this type is preserved by British Railways)	
42073 42085	2–6–4T	1945	Charles E. Fairburn	L.M.S.	General duty main line tank design developed from an earlier class of Stanier locomotives	Lakeside Railway Society, Carnforth
46443	2–6–0	1946	H. G. Ivatt	L.M.S.	Mixed traffic design for very light general duties and the forerunner of the B.R. Standard 78000 design	Severn Valley Railway, Bridgnorth
					(Other examples can be seen at The Lakeside Railway, Carnforth and Dundee Museum)	
43106	2–6–0	1947	H. G. Ivatt	L.M.S.	Light mixed traffic duties of all types	Severn Valley Railway, Bridgnorth
BLUE PETER A2 Class	4–6–2	1947	A. H. Peppercorn	L.N.E.R.	The last express passenger design prior to nationalisation and intended to become an L.N.E.R. Standard type	York Motive Power Depot.
OLIVER CROMWELL Britannia Class	4–6–2	1951	R. A. Riddles		Express passenger type and the first of the 12 standard designs to appear	Bressingham Hall, Diss, Norfolk
					(The original locomotive of this class 'Britannia' is also preserved although not at present on view)	
73050	4–6–0	1951	R. A. Riddles		The mixed traffic design derived from Stanier 5MT 4–6–0 class of the L.M.S.	Peterborough Locomotive Society, Peterborough
75027	4–6–0	1951	R. A. Riddles		The lighter weight mixed traffic design for cross country and semi-fast working	Bluebell Railway, Sussex
					(Several other members of this class have also been preserved, e.g. The Sheppard Preservation Society, Longmoor)	
80079	2–6–4T	1951	R. A. Riddles		Suburban and inter-city design also for secondary duties of a general nature	Destined for Severn Valley Railway, Bridgnorth
					(Another example is to be found on the Keighley and Worth Valley Railway)	
EVENING STAR	2–10–0	1954	R. A. Riddles		The heavy freight design was the final one before the decision to abandon steam power. The last engine appeared in 1960 and was specially named 'Evening Star'.	Not at present on view

THE IRONSTONE INDUSTRY
OF NORTHAMPTONSHIRE

General History

Iron is a mineral treasure from beneath the soil and the Northampton Sand Ironstone Bed holds the principal deposits in Britain. It is one of the three main beds of stratified ironstone of the Jurassic system which extend southwards from the Tees in the shape of a giant crescent to the coast at Weymouth. The Northampton Sand Ironstone Bed runs from central Lincolnshire across east Leicestershire, Rutland, Northamptonshire and into Oxfordshire. Chemical action in a prehistoric sea laid down this ore and it remains as the last major source of the mineral left in the country.

The origins of iron ore mining and smelting in Northamptonshire are very ancient. Men of the iron age are known to have made weapons and implements in the area, as are the Romans. By Norman times the workings were thought to be extensive and indeed one of the motivations of William the Conqueror in building Rockingham Castle was to protect the iron furnaces in the area.

For centuries charcoal was used to smelt the ore and Rockingham Forest supplied an abundance of timber. However, during the reign of Elizabeth I the depletion of the forest began to cause concern due to the competing requirements of timber for shipbuilding. Parliament subsequently passed a series of timber laws which restricted charcoal burning, and iron production in Northamptonshire gradually ceased, the smelting being moved to Staffordshire and South Wales where an abundant supply of coal could be found.

During the subsequent lapse of many years geologists often denied the existence of any vast deposits in the area despite the fact that nearly all of old Northampton was built of iron-tinged sandstone. It was not until the construction of the railways that large deposits were found. The building of the cuttings and tunnels revealed the presence of undreamt-of quantities of ore. This became publicised and set a stir amongst Victorian industrialists; samples of the ore were displayed at the Great Exhibition of 1851. The predominantly rural areas of Northamptonshire were on the brink of a great boom period.

In 1852 Thomas Butlin of Wellingborough smelted the first North-amptonshire pig-iron of the new era. The railways themselves had vastly increased the demand for iron and provided a wonderful opportunity for conveying the ore away to furnaces in the Midlands and North. The Midland Railway's main line extension southwards from Leicester ran through the heart of the iron belt and numerous pits sprang up alongside it between Market Harborough and Wellingborough to take full advantage of such a heaven-sent opportunity for conveyance.

From 1869 to 1872 output from the Northamptonshire pits exceeded 1 million tons per year and it became second only to the Cleveland district of Yorkshire in terms of production. By 1874 Butlins of Wellingborough had 4 furnaces which were producing 500 tons of pig iron per week and in addition were sending thousands of tons of ore weekly to Derbyshire and Yorkshire. More blast furnaces followed and, by 1880, 17 were in existence along with 30 separate quarries. Production soon soared past the million tons per year mark.

The industrialists were overjoyed at the richness of the earth and Wellingborough became known as the 'Iron Town'. There were predictions of it becoming a second Wolverhampton; already it was providing iron for the construction of the London Underground. A contemporary local poet wrote 'We sleep and live encased in iron, we walk on iron, we worship in walls of iron, cellars of iron keep our beer cool, and finally we are buried in iron'. The night skies began to glow with the new furnaces and the face of the county began to change.

One problem however did occur, for whilst the industrialists had the ore and the method of transportation, they did not have the coal needed for smelting. Time and time again they searched for it, schemes were drawn up, shafts were sunk and speculation was placed upon the rumours of a rich coal belt. After numerous false hopes and some bankruptcies it had to be admitted that Northamptonshire had not a piece of coal and that therefore either the iron must be brought to the coal for smelting or coal must be transported.

The original quarrying was done by landowners who eventually formed into private companies. In the very early days the ore was carried in carts drawn either by horses or manpower, but where any distance was involved the use of railway systems quickly came into being, especially since the working surfaces became further away as the quarries advanced. It was the policy from the very beginning for the quarry owners to provide their own method of transport either to the furnaces or to links with the main railway system. This was natural as theirs were private concerns and their railway systems were inevitably of a temporary nature, having neither the strength nor clearances to take normal-sized locomotives. Steam locomotives of small construction began to appear on the iron-fields. They were built by private locomotive works, many of them for narrow gauge tracks and the first is believed to have commenced work at Irthlingborough in 1867.

The success of the early quarry companies depended largely upon their accessibility to a main line railway by means of their own railway system. The ore not smelted locally was sent to Derbyshire and Nottinghamshire. The narrow gauges were favoured in view of the limited clearances in the quarries but this system necessitated the re-loading of the ore into the waggons of the main railway. Eventually many of them converted to the standard 4' 8½" thereby enabling a through operation of waggons and transfer sidings were situated at the junctions. Some, however, remained on the narrow gauge system, notably the two railways serving the Kettering and Wellingborough furnaces, as no transhipment of the mineral was required.

Originally the removal of the overburden (usually comprised of top soil, clay and limestone) was done by hand as was the filling of the carts or railway waggons. Eventually hand methods became inadequate and the first mechanical shovel for waggon loading was introduced in 1895. In 1900 the industry was revolutionised by the first steam shovels nicknamed 'American Devils'. These moved on rails and by slashing vigorously at the overburden, laid bare the ore beds. They contributed to a large increase in production and were especially useful as the extending quarries were continually encountering a deeper overburden. They came to be widely used and stalked the countryside like prehistoric monsters.

The opencast method of quarrying was generally favoured, although some underground mines were developed. Underground mining has proved to be much more costly and has often meant leaving part of the iron seam to form a safe roof whereas with the opencast method the whole of the workable ironstone bed can be won.

Booming though the industry was, it met with fierce opposition, perhaps of a kind similar to that the railways had seen many years previously. Northamptonshire has always been a beautiful county and when the scars of the iron workings became evident and more fields, woods and glades were torn up in ever increasing numbers, the county folk began to wonder if their richness in iron was perhaps a curse instead of a blessing. Quite apart from the loss in beauty was the fear that so much agricultural land would be laid to waste that the area would become impoverished and barren.

Originally the early mining had followed a three stage programme: the overburden lying above the next strip of ironstone to be worked would be used to fill in the area from which the ironstone had just been extracted, whilst the topsoil would be taken from the strip of land third in order by wheelbarrow and spread over the re-settled overburden. The restored land would then be ready to be returned for crops. As this process continued, so the quarry continued across the land, healing up its scars as it went.

Upon the advent of American Devils however, this separation of the fertile topsoil was not possible and when the filling in came to be done the land consisted of rocky ridges and hollows which rendered agriculture impossible. The desolation areas became known as 'the mountains of the moon' and were fit only for the planting of trees. Many new woods came into existence as a result of this.

This meant that with more and more land being laid to waste one treasure was being gained and another lost.

Electric shovels began to replace the American Devils, some of which were capable of stripping and disposing the overburden in one operation to a depth of 55', moving about 12 tons at a bite. These were necessary in order to cope with the ever-increasing depths of the overburden.

In 1938 the Kennett Committee was formed to investigate the land restoration problem. By this time ironstone had been taken from 3,000 acres without restoration to agriculture and a further 70,000 acres were earmarked for mining in the next 150 years, a high percentage of which it was estimated would be laid to waste. The problem became worse with the outbreak of war in 1939 and the resultant increase in demand for home ore. In 1942 the Northamptonshire County Council made a determined attempt to persuade the Government to make restoration obligatory, their object being threefold: to effect minimum loss to agriculture and rural beauty without hampering the mineral undertakings.

In 1951 the Mineral Workings Act was passed providing
1) Restoration of the land compulsory wherever possible
2) A Restoration Fund being set up by the Exchequer
3) Provision for the restoration of land laid derelict in the past.

The procedure from then on was for the operators to restore the land but to receive financial assistance from the fund if this was deemed impracticable and involved high costs.

Thus great progress was made in man's fight for beauty against ugliness and for the first time in many years the Northamptonshire people were hopeful of handing on to posterity an unblemished countryside.

As the depths of overburden increased the electric shovels became inadequate and this led to the introduction in 1951 of the first 'Walking Dragline'. In the working position the heads of the booms of the larger draglines are up to 188' – higher than Nelson's Column. They have a dumping radius of up to 280' and when slewing, the heads of the booms can reach 23 m.p.h., whilst the buckets have a capacity of up to 30 cubic yards. At night they carry lights to warn aircraft.

Understandably the entire ironstone area was quickly covered with railway systems and for many years these have provided a haven of interest for the locomotive connoisseur. One can draw similarities here with the principal railway network in pre-grouping times when each company had its own system and locomotives. Likewise the mineral companies and their locomotives came from a wide diversity of private builders and over a few square miles of good ironstone country innumerable types could be found at work.

As the years progressed they became increasingly noted as strongholds for steam locomotives of archaic designs and it appeared that for many years to come they would continue. Standardisation seemed largely to escape them and although the numerous private ironstone companies eventually became linked with much larger iron and steel concerns they still retained a multitude of locomotive types.

Unfortunately the recent decline in demand for home-produced ore in favour of imported Australian and Swedish ore combined with rationalisations within the steel industry has led to closure of many mineral workings and in some that have survived the weekly output has fallen to no more than 3,000 tons.

The decline in the demand for home ore was partly due to the high freight charges on the railway and partly because the iron content was only 28–30%, whereas the imported Swedish ore was up to 65%. Meanwhile improved methods of shipping and the expansion of steel works on the coast rendered it more economical to import than produce at home. Accordingly the succession of iron ore trains radiating away from North-amptonshire became largely a memory. The stronghold of Corby upon which most of the production became centred was the only remaining works in the county. Wellingborough Works closed in 1962, followed by Kettering in 1963. The pits that survived became dieselised quicker than was imagined and with the closure of some pits diesel locomotives were released for use in those where steam locomotives remained. However, in 1966 some 50 steam locomotives were still at work on the field.

The passing of the steam ironstone railways was a sad event and memories will long remain of the fascinating little engines puffing out of the quarries and hauling their loads of golden produce away through the woodlands and meadows.

The remains of some of the old systems can still be seen, their track-beds now overgrown and the defunct workings left to decay whilst occasionally a derelict engine, built by a firm long since forgotten, could be found rusting away amid the ever-encroaching greenery.

Where once the early ironstone companies found the remains of Roman workings so may future generations find some buried history of this once great industry. Iron is a mineral treasure and it continues to lie beneath the soil.

Corby – Centre of Northamptonshire Ironstone

It was during the building of the Midland Railway's line from Kettering to Manton in the 1870s that huge quantities of ore were revealed in the Corby district. In 1880 Mr Samuel Lloyd of Lloyd & Lloyd, the Birming-ham tube makers, visited Corby, examined the deposits and found them to be very extensive; the visit was prompted no doubt by the dwindling reserves of Staffordshire ore. This led to the formation in 1880 of the Cardigan Iron Ore Co. which leased the mineral rights from Lord Cardigan the landowner, and a standard-gauge railway was built to connect with the Midland's new route. In the first year alone over 20,000 tons of ore were despatched.

Lloyds Ironstone Co. was formed in 1885 to take over the business and extend it, and by the turn of the century three separate quarries were in operation each with its own railway system, the company owning a total of 6 locomotives. This expansion was helped by Lloyds' pioneering of a steam digger in 1895 which was a big advancement from the earlier hand shovelling.

A milestone was reached in 1910 when the company built two blast furnaces on the site alongside the original quarries, thereby making the first Corby iron. The commencement of the Great War in 1914 saw a vast increase in production, demand being so great that the railway system was extended out to Weldon, Gretton and Rockingham.

Stewarts & Lloyds came into existence after an amalgamation in 1903 of the two largest tube makers in the country, Lloyd & Lloyd of Birmingham and Stewarts & Menzies of Glasgow. Lloyds Ironstone Co. was quite separate from this arrangement, although they supplied ore to Stewarts & Lloyds for steel making. However, enterprising as ever, they desperately wanted to develop a steel works on the site at Corby and felt that a merger with the larger Stewarts & Lloyds would enable them to do this.

This was promising to become a real possibility when Stewarts & Lloyds announced a policy of expansion, being anxious to gain possession of the raw materials, and began seriously to consider the ironstone companies and a few collieries. A result of this was their purchase of the North Lincs. Ironstone Co.

Other large manufacturing concerns were doing much the same thing, however, and in consequence Lloyds Ironstone was acquired by Alfred Hickman Iron and Steel Manufacturers of Bilston, Staffordshire, in 1919. It all became settled when Stewarts & Lloyds took over Hickmans in 1920, thus acquiring Lloyds Ironstone.

Corby was chosen under the new company as the site for much of the production, as some 500 million tons of raw material were estimated to be at hand and the process of a huge operation of mining and steel tube making on the one location was envisaged. The great depression of the '20s was taking place, however, and Stewarts & Lloyds had to borrow money in order to develop the works, actually commencing in 1932. So ultimately 1934 was the first manufacture year of steel tubes in Corby.

Hitherto Corby had been little more than a sleepy village, despite the industrious Lloyds Ironstone Co., but with the announcement of the new industrial boom people converged from all over the country – Scots, Irish and many others who had been unemployed during the depression. I am acquainted with one worker who walked all the way from Cornwall.

Corby's existence was due to the Northamptonshire sand ironstone and alongside the steel works set in the heart of the farmlands a new town began to grow.

It quickly became cosmopolitan and the many different peoples combined with the vast steel works made it a wonderful yet somewhat terrifying place. At night the glow from the works could be seen for miles over the undulating countryside and became known as the 'Corby Candle'. Corby Works came into being to mine the ore, smelt it, convert the iron into steel and the steel into tubes, and as such began to play a vital role in the British steel industry.

With the new development in mind, extensions to the quarry systems came in 1930 when Stewarts & Lloyds acquired the Islip Iron Co. along with a quarry at Harringworth. The intention was to link both of these up with the Corby Works by their own railway system thereby avoiding the intermediate journey over the L.M.S. metals. The war intervened, however, Islip was never reached, and the existing furnaces there continued operation.

The line to Harringworth was eventually opened in 1952 and became a very important part of the system, some special 30-ton steel hopper waggons being specially built for it.

Corby Works played a very great part in the second world war and succeeded in manufacturing vast quantities of pipeline which was urgently needed for supplies. After the war intentions were announced of developing Corby even further, and in 1949 commencement was made upon more extensions to the works. The expansion programme continued and during the decade up to 1970, £48 million were spent to procure a larger and better production.

In 1950 Corby was designated a new town and a development corporation was set up. The influence that the Steel Industry had upon Corby is summarised by the following table.

Population in	1930	1500
	1951	25000
	1970	50000

After the nationalisation of the steel industry in 1968 Stewarts & Lloyds eventually became known as the Corby Works of the Tubes Division of the British Steel Corporation. The works have continued to flourish and have become the largest of their kind in Europe, and by 1970 employed 12,000 people, possessing an annual tube-making capacity of almost 1 million tons. Technological advances and many forms of sophisticated instrumentation have ensured that Corby will for long remain at the forefront of one of Britain's greatest industries.

The operations at the steel works are as fascinating as they are exciting. The raw ore comes by rail into the North Bank exchange sidings which constitute a dividing line between the mines operation and the steel division. From there it goes to the giant crushing plant to be mixed with coke, and thence to the sinter plant where the coke and ore are burned to a clinker. The works have two coke oven plants which provide the fuel for the sintering process. It is this clinker which is fed to the blast furnaces and the resulting molten iron is run off whilst the slag and waste, which is of a lighter nature, rises to the top of the giant cauldrons.

The next stage is the passing of the raw iron to the steel furnaces for the further removal of carbon and the addition of alloying elements, the combination producing the steel. One of the truly exciting sights of the works is of the huge ladles of molten iron being trundled around on the internal railway system.

The steel is poured into ingot moulds and left to cool prior to despatch to the rolling mills for manufacture into bars. The ingots are reheated to a temperature of 1300°C and reduced to bars. The bars are further reduced to strips which eventually pass to the tube mills where the manufacture of tubes to specification is undertaken. A flying saw cuts the tubes to length amid a dazzling array of fire and sparks.

The tubes have a wide diversity of uses, many being required for water, gas or steam in important installations all over the world. Northamptonshire ore is especially suitable for tube-making and ore which days previously lay deep in the earth is ready for despatch by rail as tubes.

With such a vast undertaking in steel production the quarries flourished and in 1950 a separate company was set up under the name of Stewarts & Lloyds Minerals Ltd. to look after the vast quarrying interests. Upon the formation of this company the manufacturing side became known as the Steel Division.

The advent of the Walking Dragline enabled deeper quarries to be worked and after the closure of the Harringworth quarries a new one was commenced at Oakley only two miles away from the works. It was here that the giant W1800 Dragline came to be situated and it has raised large quantities of ore from up to 100' below the surface. Accordingly, the tendency over recent years has been to quarry closer to the steel works than was previously possible.

The previously mentioned decline in demand for Northamptonshire ore has applied to such companies as Richard Thomas and Baldwin and South Durham Iron and Steel, whose works situated near to the coast have turned partly to richer imported ore. Corby, however, has continued to produce the cheapest ore in Britain because of its perfect situation on the ore beds.

Although a little mineral continues to be transported away from Northamptonshire, Corby remains a gigantic living memorial to the halcyon days when the night skies glowed red all across the county's orefields and the sounds of ironstone activity rang from Wellingborough, Kettering, Cranford, Islip and so many other places.

The Locomotives of Corby—Minerals Division

The first locomotive to work the Corby ironstone systems was for the Cardigan Company and arrived in 1883. It was of the 0–4–0ST type. By the beginning of the twentieth century 7 locomotives were at work, including the first 0–6–0ST which was later to become the basic type over the ensuing 70 years. The first of these 0–6–0STs arrived in 1903 and was a Hudswell Clarke which was named *Pen Green* after one of the early quarries. Tank engines were necessary for these systems and completely suitable. They offered sufficient adhesion without too much excess weight, an important factor since the trains of ironstone were heavy and fierce gradients were inevitably a part of the sinuous systems.

It is of great interest that the Manning Wardle 0–6–0STs became the standard locomotives for the quarry systems; the basic design was used until 1941 and could be traced directly back to the first locomotive of 1910 which later became No. 38. Two further locomotives of similar design were received second-hand in 1912, later becoming Nos. 34 & 35 respectively. Further new examples were obtained from Mannings in 1921.

After the demise of Manning Wardle in 1927 further locomotives were obtained from Kitson & Co. who had taken over Manning's goodwill. As late as 1941 more locomotives of this type were obtained from Robert Stephenson & Hawthorns who had by then taken over the goodwill of Kitsons and with it that of Manning Wardle. As the illustrations show, the design remained practically the same regardless of builder, which is sufficient evidence of the very high regard that the Corby men, having used the type for almost 60 years, had for these splendid locomotives.

After 1911 locomotives were purchased for duties in the ironworks and there became in effect two fleets. Accordingly, in 1936 a renumbering scheme was introduced whereby the iron and steel works locomotives were numbered 1 to 30 and the quarry locomotives from 31 upwards. Both systems were numbered in building date order.

Just before the Second World War the company's intention of linking Islip led to their ordering 8 0–6–0STs of the 50550 Class from the Hunslet Engine Co. These, although constructed to Stewarts & Lloyds requirements, were not needed after the abandonment of the Islip project; only one was ever destined to work at Corby, and this rather surprisingly went to the steel works where it remained the only one of its type.

In 1950 7 large 0–6–0STs were delivered from Robert Stephenson and Hawthorn. These were the 56 Class 18″ inside-cylinder locomotives which were also built after collaboration with Stewarts & Lloyds Minerals in order to meet their special requirements. They were of similar appearance to the Hunslet Austerity type and were intended for the extensions out to Cowthick and Harringworth. These locomotives arrived in green livery with red side rods and led to the adoption of that colour scheme for all the mineral engines. Two further locomotives to this design arrived in 1954 and 1958 respectively. (Plate nos. 111, 112 and 116.)

A common engine shed had been in use from 1934 to 1954 but after the formation of the Minerals Division a new 8-road depot was constructed at Pen Green along with an adjacent locomotive works which undertook major overhauls. It was to this depot that all engines engaged upon quarry work were transferred. The original depot and workshops came solely under the Steel Division.

In 1960 the 25 locomotives allocated to Pen Green were:

No.	Name	Builder	Type	Date Built
34	CALETTWR ⎫		0–6–0ST	1895
35	RHIWNANT ⎬ Manning Wardle		etc.	
38	DOLOBRAN ⎭			1910
39	RHOS	Hudswell Clarke		1918 (Outside Cylinders)
41	RHYL ⎫ Manning Wardle			1921
42	RHONDDA ⎭			1921
44	CONWAY ⎫			1933
45	COLWYN ⎪			1933
46	CARDIGAN ⎬ Kitson (M.W. Design)			1934
47	CARNARVON ⎪			1934
48	CRIGGION ⎭			1936
49	CAERPHILLY ⎫			1936
52	⎪ Robert Stephenson & Hawthorn			1940
53	⎬ (M.W. Design)			1941
54	⎪			1941
55	⎭			1941
56	⎫			1950
57	⎪ Robert Stephenson & Hawthorn			1950
58	⎬ (18″ Tanks built to S. & L.			1950
59	⎭ specification)			1950

No. Name	Builder	Type	Date Built
60	⎫	0-6-0ST	1950
61	⎪ Robert Stephenson & Hawthorn		1950
62	⎬ (18″ Tanks built to S. & L.		1950
63	⎪ specification)		1954
64	⎭		1958

It will be noticed that those built prior to 1940 carried names of Welsh towns, some of which were in deference to the Welsh connections of the Lloyd family.

The use of inside-cylinder locomotives for quarry operations was the rule for many years due to the increased clearances offered by this design.

The Manning Wardle design locomotives were used in the quarries to a very great extent, especially in the more restricted ones where their smaller size was an advantage. The permanent way and equipment trains were also a Manning Wardle duty. These were frequently necessary all over the system as the track continually had to be slewed in order to follow the ever-varying course of the diggers.

It is this fact that makes the study of old mineral railways so difficult; owing to the perpetual slewing of tracks and filling up of the old quarries for land restoration, maps very quickly become out of date.

The larger Robert Stephenson and Hawthorn 18″ engines worked the longer journeys and in later years were often found taking loaded ironstone trains down to the North Bank exchange sidings.

The journey of a loaded mineral train from the digger at the pit face up to the exchange sidings for the steel works was truly fascinating and the pleasure of watching these systems at work will not easily be forgotten. Dawn each morning saw the first locomotives away from Pen Green sheds, each designated either for one of the pits, for shunting operations at the exchange sidings or for permanent way and equipment trains.

The countryside for miles around resounded with the bark of their exhausts as they laboured out through the deep gashes in the earth along the crude tracks and away across the woodlands and fields. When bringing in the empties they would idly clank their waggons up to the digger at the working face, to return later amid a storm of drama with the loads of golden produce.

It was a joy to spend a summer's day on these mineral systems where in between trains the quietness of the surrounding countryside was a deep pleasure, especially in a county so renowned for its wild life.

The hope that these delightful locomotives would remain at Pen Green was dashed soon after the nationalisation of steel in 1968 when the programme of dieselisation was completed. Many of the intruders were the British Rail Class 14 hydraulics which, after being displaced, were sold to British Steel.

One by one the steam engines were withdrawn until in November 1968 only 6 remained in service, and in January 1969 steam working came to an end, to the dismay of locomotive enthusiasts the country over. This was not, however, to be the last word; preservation societies quickly moved in, for the size of these engines rendered them a possibility for groups with limited funds. Some of the results that the societies achieved follow under 'Preserved Ironstone Locomotives'.

The Steel Division

After Lloyds built the first ironworks in 1910 it was found necessary to acquire locomotives for operations around the new furnaces. Consequently, the following year saw the arrival of two Andrew Barclay 0–6–0STs named *Ironworks No. 1* and *No. 2* respectively, one of which survived until 1961. A further locomotive, *Ironworks No. 3,* arrived from Hudswell Clarke in 1919.

The Steelworks also used the 0–6–0ST type and the extensions made in 1934 necessitated a great increase in power which led to the arrival in that year of 6 Hawthorn Leslie 0–6–0STs with outside cylinders and it was this type that was to become the most prevalent. These were followed in 1936–37 by a further four locomotives. In 1940–41 two more locomotives of the same design were acquired from the Robert Stephenson and Hawthorn Co., the result of the amalgamation between Hawthorne Leslie and Robert Stephenson & Co. (Plate no. 117.)

During the war years the continued expansion of production brought several second-hand locomotives to the works, some of vintage design. An interesting example was an ex-Caledonian Railway 0–4–0ST Pug which had passed into L.M.S. stock as No. 16037 and was received by Stewarts & Lloyds from a colliery in Hamilton in 1945. This was a typical example of the numerous small pre-grouping designs that were sold to various industrial concerns.

Also during this period the inside-cylinder 50550 Class 0–6–0ST arrived from Hunslet – one of the 8 originally meant for the Islip extension.

Unlike the quarry locomotives, outside-cylinder types have always been preferred for engines used in the works, for the debris which tended to fall onto the tracks would damage the working parts of an inside-cylinder design.

The separation of the minerals and steel divisions in 1950 led to yellow being adopted as the standard livery for the works locomotives which rendered them much more easily seen amongst the gloomy structures. The Hawthorn Leslie 0–6–0ST may be regarded as the standard type and the beginning of 1970 saw 9 of them left in service along with the larger Hunslet 50550 class 0–6–0ST.

When delivered, the Hawthorn Leslies were traditional coal burners but in the early 1960s Stewarts & Lloyds adopted a policy of converting many of them to burn Britoleum oil. This was a result of the serious shortage of suitable coal at that time. Quite apart from overcoming the coal problem this conversion gave a number of additional advantages, the principal one being increased availability, for steam could be raised within 1 hour whereas 3 had been necessary with coal. Furthermore, no fire cleaning or bunkering up was necessary. The oil entered the firebox in the form of a spray and could be operated either by steam or compressed air. One marked disadvantage was that if the locomotive was left unattended the boiler pressure fell rapidly. No. 21 as illustrated was retained as a coal burner.

The works locomotives have been very active since 1911 and although their functions differed greatly from those of the quarry engines they were none the less fascinating. They were responsible for bringing in raw materials from the connections with British Railways, which included huge loads of limestone, coal and slack needed for the making of steel. One of their more interesting duties was to transfer the ladles of molten iron from the blast furnaces to the steel plant and the sight of them hauling the huge cauldrons of red hot iron against the background of the works was enthralling. After the manufacture of iron into steel ingots it would again be transferred by rail, this time up to the rolling mills to be made into bars.

Other locomotives would be found feeding coal into the large coke ovens or trundling the loads of slag from the furnaces round to the asphalt plant for the manufacture of tar-macadam. They performed a similar operation with the slag from the steel plant which was taken away for the manufacture of fertilisers. After processing they would be summoned to struggle out of the works with a load of completed tubes to be handed over at the exchange sidings with B.R.

The sounds of their endeavours amid the clamours of the steel works could be heard all over Corby as they rumbled from plant to plant, silhouetted against a fiery background of orange incandescence.

During 1969 the final important overhauls to the remaining steam locomotives were undertaken and 1970 saw only 6 in regular daily operation, the remainder of the work being undertaken by diesels which were preferred for their higher availability and power.

It has been estimated that several of the Hawthorn Leslie 0-6-0STs may survive until 1971, which would give them the distinction of being the last steam locomotives to remain in service on the Lincolnshire–Oxfordshire iron belt.

Nassington, Northamptonshire - Focus on an Ironstone Pit

As one leaves the main A47 road from Uppingham to Peterborough at the Wandsford turn a few miles' journey brings one to the delightful Northamptonshire village of Nassington. Tucked away amid wooded farmland the village appears to be very much as any other in the area, built in the typical local limestone and slumbering peacefully on either side of the secondary road that passes through it.

In the early months of 1970, however, Nassington exhibited a distinction that made it unique not only in Northamptonshire but in the whole of Britain. This distinction centred on the Nassington Barrowden Mining Co. Ltd., whose ironstone quarries were the last privately-owned ones to remain in existence and were also the final stronghold of steam power.

The hasty traveller of the '70s may well have failed to observe or hear the two Saddle Tank engines at work as they ambled through the woodlands the iron ore tippler waggons trundling behind and the plumes of white exhaust rising high above the surrounding meadows.

A few years ago Nassington would have been typical of many such places in the area but by this time it had become a working piece of history.

Naylor Benzon and Co. Ltd., one of Britain's largest importers of foreign ore, are the parent company and the quarries at Nassington represented their first attempt to mine home iron ore. After carefully prospecting the area they found it to be richer than hitherto supposed and they commenced mining operations in 1939.

Two locomotives were purchased from the Hunslet Engine Co., Leeds, to their 16″ 0–6–0ST design of 1923 with inside cylinders. The first arrived in October 1939 and the second in February 1940 and they were named *Jacks Green* and *Ring Haw* respectively, after two nearby woods. They were decked in green livery with red and black edging.

This was a new and exciting venture for Naylor Benzon and the concurrent outbreak of war led to a great demand for their produce. The rival company of Stewarts and Lloyds hastily bought up land to the south in an endeavour to contain the Nassington quarries within a limited area, but once mining operations began, Naylor Benzon realised that a vast tonnage of good quality ore was to be had in the immediate locality.

The first digger employed was a prototype of the walking dragline and was built by Ransome and Rapier Co. Ltd., of Ipswich. From this were later developed the famous W1400 and W1800, of which the latter was to be one of the largest in Europe.

During the vital war years ore was collected from the exchange sidings by the L.M.S.R. whose ex-L.N.W.R. line from Rugby to Peterborough ran adjacent to the quarry. It was conveyed to Scunthorpe, Scotland and Dagenham where Fords have their own blast furnaces.

Originally an overburden of only 10′ was encountered but this was eventually to increase to 65′ as the workings developed. It was discovered that Naylor Benzon were not the first people to extract the Nassington ore as the several old Roman workings that were found clearly indicated.

In 1941 an important operation commenced when large quantities of the ore were calcinated prior to despatching. The calcination of ironstone began in the Midlands in 1924 and the object of the process was to burn off moisture and gases to increase the iron content. This was especially necessary during the wartime period as it improved the quality and led to a reduction in transport, weight and costs of some 30%. Nassington ore was 30% iron and this processing increased it to 45%.

The calcination of ore has been practised in many of the Northamptonshire pits and one of the early methods was to remove the overburden, blast the ore bed and then spread slack over the fragmented pieces to a depth of several inches. The excavator then turned the ironstone and slack behind itself and deposited it onto a prepared 9″ foundation of large lump coal. The coal was ignited and the mass left to burn and smoulder for two to three months. But it was found that by using the pit method, production was liable to be held up and the clamp method was devised to avoid this.

This involved laying out sets of parallel railway lines about 90' apart and 300 yards long on an area isolated from the pit. After blasting, the raw ironstone was loaded into internal skip waggons which consisted of three detachable boxes each holding approximately 5 tons. Trains of 8–10 waggons were hauled from the ironstone workings to the site of the clamps where 9″ of large lump coal was laid on the ground. A predetermined quantity of slack coal was either deposited on the loaded skip boxes or placed inside before loading, and a crane lifted each skip and deposited it onto the lump coal. After the coal was ignited the clamps were built up to a height of 30' and left to burn for up to three months. Each clamp, or bank as they were often known, would hold up to 30,000 tons of ore. The way in which Nassington incorporated the clamp method into the system may be seen from the accompanying map.

The modern method of removing moisture and gases from the ironstone is by sintering processes at the furnaces and this is more efficient. Nassington was the last pit in Great Britain to calcine its ore, continuing until 1969.

The original pit as shown on the map was operated until 1949, after which a working fault was encountered and a new lease of land was taken which became pit number two. This eventually reached territory that had previously been earmarked by Richard Thomas and Baldwin Ltd.

Apart from selling iron ore the company also dealt in limestone, silica white sand and silica clay, commodities that were removed from the overburden. Restoration of the land at Nassington has been quite considerable and, as the clay was taken out of the surface, the fertility of the reclaimed land was improved owing to its superior drainage ability, especially when sands were introduced beneath the soil.

Life at the ironstone quarry seemingly went on at a steady rural pace, for although the weekly tonnage was often very high there was always time for a friendly word. Nassington, in common with many other ironstone concerns, had its share of personalities. Among these was Bill Evans who took over *Ring Haw* when it was new in 1940 and has driven it ever since. Bill, a real veteran of the steam age, was still at work on *Ring Haw* as he approached his 70th year, and he had for many years been instrumental in looking after the maintenance of both engines. He began his career in 1915 on steam road waggons, after which he joined the L.N.W.R. as a fireman. This was followed by a period on steam rollers before he made acquaintance with Naylor Benzon and *Ring Haw*. With 55 years of working experience, Bill could tell many tales of the steam age and it was my pleasure to ride with him upon many happy occasions.

Both engines were maintained in immaculate condition internally and externally. Perhaps the special shine on *Jacks Green* was the influence of Jim Hopkins who took her over in 1939 and subsequently drove her over the Nassington systems for more than 30 years.

In 1963 both locomotives underwent heavy overhauls and at this time a third engine was purchased second-hand from Stanton Ironworks Co. Ltd. This was an 0-6-0ST named *Buccleuch* which had been built by Peckett in 1910. For some years the three engines were used with *Buccleuch* acting as standby, but by 1968 she was regarded as superfluous and was broken up on the site. (Plate nos. 123, 124, 126, 127.)

177

Owing to the rail network being slewed to follow the workings, only one section of the quarry remained unchanged. It was here that the office, exchange sidings, locomotive depot, workshops and weighbridge were situated. No single loaded waggon was permitted to exceed 27 tons and each had to pass over the weighbridge on its journey from the pit to the exchange sidings. This meant some experienced calculations on the part of the digger operator as an excess load would have to be shunted out of the train and reduced to conformity. This did not happen very often at Nassington.

In 1967 pit number two reached the end of its working life and a new one was commenced on the opposite side of the then British Rail line from Rugby to Peterborough. It was at first thought that lorry haulage would have to be employed up to the calcine banks in order to cross the B.R. metals, thereby rendering one of the locomotives redundant. However, the Beeching Plan brought the closure of the B.R. line and Naylor Benzon obtained a lease over a section of the route. This enabled them to extend their railway system down into pit number three from one of the calcine banks by using the outer track. The Nassington to Peterborough section of this line remained open, however, for shipment of the ore which by this time was being sent to the furnaces at Scunthorpe.

The development of this pit necessitated a sharp incline of 1 in 50 up to

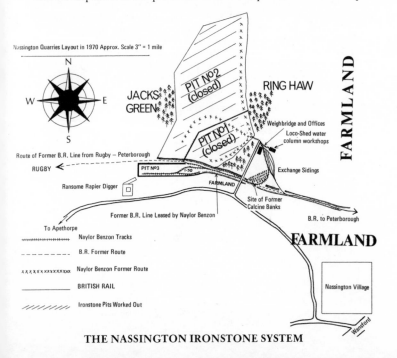

THE NASSINGTON IRONSTONE SYSTEM

the old B.R. route and 120 tons was the maximum that one locomotive could successfully operate, which led to the frequent use of both engines on one train over this stretch.

Concurrently with the opening of pit number three came the nationalisation of the Steel Industry which left Naylor Benzon with only one market and a fixed tariff for their ore. The result was a decline in demand and by 1969 only 3,000 tons per week were required. The great furnaces at Scunthorpe were being fed by the higher grade Swedish ore together with that from the Frodingham bed. It became obvious that Nassington could not continue for much longer on such a basis. The quarry was operative for only three days per week, whilst B.R. were obliged to maintain the line east from Nassington for some six trainloads weekly. It was announced that Nassington would have to close at the end of 1970 and so a long tradition ended.

The management and men had for long had great pride in their system and the news came as a blow – seemingly the end of yet another local industry. For the railway enthusiasts too it was a great disappointment as no longer would *Ring Haw* and *Jacks Green* be found in this rural retreat.

The memories will nevertheless remain for all who knew the system; indeed how could anyone forget the sound of *Ring Haw*'s exhaust as it echoed through the woods on a warm summer's morning, or the cries of the game birds as they rose up in front of the trains. It was a friendly and rustic system, no superficialities ever being necessary since iron mining is a basic business, and therein lay Nassington's intrinsic charm.

Silence will return to Nassington, the workings will be no more and the land will be restored to agriculture. The management has expressed a wish that a preservation society will purchase *Ring Haw* and *Jacks Green* in the hope that these two veterans of the pits will continue to be enjoyed by future generations.

Locomotive	Type	Builder	Date Built	General Details	Place of Preservation
Kettering Furnaces No. 3	0-4-0ST	Black Hawthorn	1885	Operated on the narrow gauge system which connected the Kettering Furnaces with the quarries	Penrhyn Castle Museum, Bangor
SIR BERKELEY	0-6-0ST	Manning Wardle	1891	Acquired by Cranford Ironstone Co. in 1934	Keighley and Worth Valley Railway
No. 35	0-6-0ST	Manning Wardle	1895	The basic design for the Corby quarries and one of the first two locomotives to arrive second hand in 1912	Foxfield Light Railway, Dilhorne, Staffs.
HENRY CORT	0-4-0ST	Peckett and Sons	1903	Donated by Richard Thomas and Baldwin for preservation after working their quarries at Irthlingborough	Foxfield Light Railway, Dilhorne, Staffs.
Kettering Furnaces No. 8	0-6-0ST	Manning Wardle	1906	Another Kettering Furnaces locomotive of larger design	Alongside the Corporation Library, Kettering
SIR THOMAS No. 1	0-6-0T	Hudswell Clarke	1918	From the Oxfordshire Ironstone Co., Banbury	London Railway Preservation Society, Quainton Road Station, Bucks.
PIXIE	0-4-0ST	W. Bagnall	1919	Narrow gauge locomotive from Cranford Pits (at one time two gauges were in use at Cranford)	Cadeby Light Railway, Market Bosworth, Leics.
STAMFORD	0-6-0ST	Avonside	1927	Ex-Staveley Mineral Pilton Quarry, Rutland	Bluebell Railway, Sussex
A Standard Peckett Design adapted for metre gauge No. 85	0-6-0ST	Peckett and Sons	1934	One of three locomotives used on the Wellingborough Ironworks system until 1966	Bressingham Hall, Diss, Norfolk
No. 16	0-6-0ST	Hawthorn Leslie	1934	Standard design from Corby Steel Works	Hunts Mineral Waters, Hinckley, Leics.
CAERNARVON	0-6-0ST	Kitson	1934	Purchased from Stewarts and Lloyds, Pen Green, Corby	Severn Valley Railway, Bridgnorth
CRANFORD No. 2	0-6-0ST	W. Bagnall	1942	Purchased from Staveley Minerals' Pits at Cranford	Overstone Park, Northants.
CHERWELL	0-6-0ST	W. Bagnall	1942	Ex-Byfield Quarry	Daventry Town Centre
Nos. 57, 62, 63	0-6-0ST	Robert Stephenson and Hawthorn	1950 1954 1954	Purchased from Stewarts and Lloyds, Corby	Keighley and Worth Valley Railway
No. 9	0-4-0ST	Andrew Barclay	1952	Locomotive from the Irchester Quarries of the South Durham Iron and Steel Co.	Irchester Village, Northants.
JUNO	0-6-0ST	Hunslet	1958	The famous Hunslet Austerity type of which some 484 were built and some are still at work. This locomotive was built for Stewarts and Lloyds Minerals Ltd.	London Railway Preservation Society, Quainton Road Station, Bucks.

(Other locomotives of this class may be found on the Keighley and Worth Valley Railway and the Dinting Railway Centre.)

The above list may serve as a guide to some places where interesting Ironstone Locomotives may be seen. It is not intended to be comprehensive and many others are preserved in various places throughout the country.

THE COAL INDUSTRY AND THE STEAM LOCOMOTIVE

*Coal and Steam – the
Lifeblood of the
Industrial Revolution*

The Industrial Revolution could never have taken place without coal and in turn the coal could barely have been made generally available without steam and the railways. The truth is that steam as a form of both power and locomotion developed in the midst of coal and it appears that it will die there too, for the majority of today's steam locomotives are still to be found eking out their existence amid the coalfields.

Coal is a gift from countless centuries ago when no eye of intelligence could gaze upon the pristine beauties of a vegetation so luxurious and dense. Far from wasting their fascinations the forests set in motion an efficient process culminating in a glorious though distant treasure when the teeming organisms were sealed down into the earth, transmuted into coal and conserved for the use of people in remote future ages.

Great Britain has the largest reserves of coal in Western Europe with the exception of the Ruhr area of Germany and the formation of seams of so great an extent indicates the past existence of forests of enormous size and their maintenance as a source of material over a long period of years.

Evidence shows that coal was used in the flint age and it was certainly used during Roman times. By A.D. 800 it had domestic uses although the utility of coal was considerably overshadowed by the abundance of wood which was so much easier to obtain.

The north east of England has for long been noted for its richness in coal and in 1259 King Henry III granted a charter for the people of Newcastle to commence the first primitive mines. This led to increasing use of the 'fossil fuel,' as it was then known, and to a public outcry against its pollutive effects; accordingly King Edward I issued a proclamation limiting its use. This prejudice was eventually broken down and by the fourteenth century coal was being extracted near the outcrops of all principal coal belts and collieries were opened in Northumberland and Durham.

In 1368 the Bishop of Durham appointed a Mines Supervisor and the first coals were shipped away from Sunderland to London, where by 1400 the new material was being very widely burned.

As the industry developed so the mines became deeper and horse power was necessary to raise the coal. Mines were constructed on both banks of the Rivers Tyne and Wear as the only means of conveyance was by water. A result of this was the development of the great Newcastle-to-London East Coast coal route and it saw the first of the thousands of coal boats that were to ply that route over the succeeding centuries. Fullest use had to be made of the coal that was adjacent to water for the heavy mineral was impossible to transport across land and an inland colliery would be limited to supplying only a small local market.

It was in such circumstances and environments that the first railways appeared and during the early seventeenth century wooden waggon ways were developed to aid transportation to the water's edge. The waggons had four flanged wheels and were hauled by horses – sometimes preceded by a man carrying a bale of hay to encourage the horse to greater efforts. If it were possible the loaded waggons would be allowed to run down to the staithes by force of gravity and, after emptying them, the horses would haul them back up the incline to the colliery. The wooden rails of these systems were found to have a very short life and after 1767 they were replaced by cast-iron.

The increasing use of coal in a developing industry combined with the constant diminution of the woodlands inevitably meant that the collieries had to be situated further from the water where the richer seams so often lay; some of the early railways which resulted reached a length of 12 miles.

Steam and coal first became connected with Newcomen's steam pumping engine used for removing water from the ever-deepening mines and by the mid-eighteenth century over 100 were at work in the north-east area alone. These were greatly improved upon by James Watt in 1784.

Continuous improvements were made in mining techniques and yet the industrial mushroom was prevented from growing owing to the impossibility of transporting coal and merchandise successfully across land. An indication of the desperate need for inland communications is shown in the fact that to smelt one ton of iron some 10 tons of material – principally coal – was necessary.

If the use of oceans and rivers was the only method of overcoming the problem the water had to lie across the land and it was in the mid-eighteenth century that a network of canals over Britain was envisaged. Construction rapidly followed and limited though the process was, the new navigation opened up industries and coal became used for iron smelting, pottery manufacture, fuel for the steam looms in the huge cotton industries and furthermore enjoyed a wider domestic usage.

It was during these years of canal development that the steam locomotive was born for work on the iron waggon way of the collieries. The birth came with Richard Trevethick's locomotive for the Pen-y-daren Colliery in South Wales and although it rapidly broke up the cast-iron rails it successfully hauled 15 tons of coal at 5 m.p.h. Further engines followed and Trevethick was commissioned to build others, one of which was for Wylam Colliery near Newcastle. Perhaps the most successful of the early locomotives were those of the Middleton Tramway which had been authorised in 1758 to build a $3\frac{1}{2}$-mile waggon way for conveying coal into Leeds city. In 1812 they converted to haulage by steam loco-motives designed by a prominent engineer named Murray who used the rack system as patented by Blenkinsop. This method added teeth to the driving wheels; these fitted cogs on the rails and thus prevented slipping. This proved, however, to be an unnecessary precaution: these engines were able to haul almost 100 tons of coal and, when returning with the empty waggons, reached 10 m.p.h.

The great news of the 'Iron Horses' spread and many collieries turned to locomotives, the 19th of which was George Stephenson's first engine, named *Blücher,* for the Killingworth Colliery. However, the revolution truly commenced when the owners of collieries at Darlington wished to transport their excellent coal down to the coast and George Stephenson was commissioned to build the line. Initially the owners felt that horse power would suffice but Stephenson quickly dispensed with such nonsense. He wrote –

'The strength of Great Britain lies in her iron and coal beds and above all other agencies the locomotive is destined to bring it forth. The Lord Chancellor now sits upon a bag of wool but wool has long ceased to be emblematical of the staple commodity of England. He ought to sit upon a bag of coals.'

The Stockton and Darlington was a public railway and it enabled the steam locomotive and the railway to emerge from the collieries and present themselves to a world that within a very few years they were to revolutionise completely.

So truly commenced the great industrial age: rich new inland collieries were opened up by the railways to meet the ever-growing demand for coal and the iron furnaces and factories multiplied as the nation exploited its wealth. The exploitation was made by a people endowed with in-domitable energy and intelligence which enabled Britain to take front place amongst the world's nations.

During the 1820s export of coal increased and the huge demand for production was aided by two developments in mining, the introduction of the safety lamp in 1815 and the use of steam power for raising up coals and for driving ventilation fans. These developments enabled mines to be struck deeper and therefore more economically.

The increase in national coal production may be seen by the following table.

Year	Annual Tonnage Raised in Millions of Tons
1750	5
1830	22
1836	30
1850	60
1861	84
1866	100
1891	185
1900	225
*1913	287

* (This figure indicates the maximum output ever achieved, 77 million tons of which were exported)

The 1866 figure was the result of 4,000 collieries and of the total produced London alone took 6 million tons, while a further 7 million were exported. It was also estimated at that time that 1,000 blast furnaces were in operation, manufacturing some 5 million tons of iron which had by this date all been smelted with coal. Further to this was the reliance on coal of manufacturing establishments, gasworks, steam locomotives, ocean steamers and domestic needs. So great was the dependence at that time that fears were expressed for the days when the coalfields would yield no more. Many dates and estimates were brandished about and there were calls for conservation.

After 1913 a decline in production was suffered over the war years, partly owing to a reduction in exports, and when the war was over electricity began to compete in home and factory, whilst the huge coal-burning ships were fast turning to oil. Exports continued to decline as foreign consumers developed their own resources whilst improved smelting techniques further reduced the demand for coal production. These factors coupled with continual labour problems within the coal industry led to a decline to 207 million tons in 1933.

The advent of the diesel engine and piped natural gas was further to accelerate the decline with the inevitable result that numerous collieries had to be closed.

So may be seen the rise and decline of a vast and complex industry and how the railway and the steam engine rose and declined in accordance. Despite modernisation of the industry, steam locomotives may still be found on many colliery systems and these true descendants of Trevethick's locomotive of 1804 still hand over the coals to the huge diesel locomotives of British Rail, although needless to say they are now a fast dying race.

Much of the mining in Northumberland today is centred around Ashington which is an excellent place to observe the final years of a tradition almost 2 centuries old.

Ashington, Northumberland – Focus on a Colliery System

The royalties worked by the Ashington Coal Company lay to the north of the River Wansbeck between the N.E.R.'s portion of the East Coast main line and the sea. They were leased from several owners and occupied a total area of 37 square miles, 14 of which were under the sea.

In 1850 the first colliery at Ashington was opened and a line was put in to link with the N.E.R.'s route to Blyth.

In 1866 the first shaft was sunk at Ashington and was known as the 'Bothal'; this proved to be the commencement of a rapid development and by the 1920s five fully equipped collieries were in operation; a total annual output of some $3\frac{1}{2}$ million tons was achieved by the mid 1930s.

The collieries were as under:

	Location	Approx. Daily Output (Mid 1930s)
Ashington	Centre of operations	5000 tons
Linton	2 miles north	1900 tons
Ellington	$2\frac{1}{2}$ miles north-east	2500 tons
Lynemouth	$2\frac{1}{2}$ miles north-east	1000 tons
Woodhorn	$1\frac{1}{2}$ miles east	2600 tons

The marketable products consisted of high class, cleaned and graded coal for both domestic and steam-raising uses. The former was known as 'Ashington Wallsend' and 'Bothal House' whilst the steam coal was called 'Bothal West Hartley'. Some of the pits were so long that they necessitated extra shafts in order to place the men adjacent to the working face, thereby saving a long walk underground.

Originally all coals were transported away by the North Eastern Railway but in later years this changed to the London & North Eastern Railway and British Railways in turn and by the time that the latter had come into being, Ashington had passed into the Northumberland Area of the National Coal Board.

During the great export days, much of Ashington's coal was shipped away from Blyth which was the natural port of shipment for the East Northumberland Coalfield. Blyth has always dealt principally in coal. This port was specially equipped to handle a vast tonnage and had 140 acres of deep water area with waiting berths for 40 vessels of up to 12,000 tons dead weight capacity and its shipping equipment was capable of dealing with 7 million tons per annum. The Ashington Coal Company had its shipping office on the North Staiths and sent large quantities to Poland, Sweden and Germany.

The route to Blyth was via Sleekburn and Cambois. Coals sent to South Blyth were despatched via Bedlington through to Newsham, at which point the locomotive ran round its train and proceeded northwards up to Blyth. The only time that South Blyth was used was to relieve pressure on other parts of the harbour and enable a quicker turn round for the ships. Other coals went to the Tyne and across country to Silloth.

In addition to its export trade, the company sold a large tonnage for home use, including 'steam coal' which was sent to many locomotive sheds throughout the country.

Ashington was the administrative centre for the company and by the mid 1930s 8,600 people were employed. The company possessed 15 route miles of railway in addition to 9 miles of sidings which gave a storage capacity for some 35,000 tons of coal. A total of 750 waggons were owned and 17 steam locomotives were required to operate the system.

The entire area was reliant solely upon the richness of its coal belts and Ashington was a true 'Coal Town' whilst the adjacent village of Lynemouth was built by the company to house the colliery workers. In addition to its mining activities, the company farmed many acres of royalty land and provided much of the foodstuffs for the community.

The railway system shown by the map developed over a period of years and the first important part was the Ashington to Longhirst Junction section which was opened in 1866. This enabled coals bound for Tyne Dock at Newcastle to be transported up the East Coast main line.

In 1895 the line to Linton Colliery was built and N.E.R. locomotives were permitted on to the system to enable them to connect with Blyth so that through workings could be operated.

In 1909 the line was extended by the company to Ellington Colliery and again N.E.R. locomotives worked onto the system from Blyth. 1923 saw further extensions when the Ellington to Lynemouth Shore section was opened, although it was not until 1937 that engines of other than the Ashington companies reached this point.

Ashington and Woodhorn Collieries had been linked by the N.E.R.'s line from Blyth to Newbiggin but in 1930 the company constructed their own line to Woodhorn which ran parallel to the North Eastern's, for although N.E.R. locomotives were permitted on to the Ashington system the Ashington locomotives were confined to their own metals.

The colliery at Newbiggin owned by Bainbridge was a separate concern and did not become incorporated into the system until after nationalisation when it was joined by rail with Lynemouth in 1964. A few years prior to this, in 1956, Woodhorn and Lynemouth had been linked by a double line for both British Railways and colliery traffic.

Other noteworthy extensions after nationalisation were those out to Coneygarth Drift in 1949 and to Longhirst Drift in 1956.

The precise layout and settings of the various routes may be seen on the accompanying map.

Apart from the coal traffic, the company commenced a passenger service over the Ashington to Linton route in 1895. This was later extended to Ellington and was fascinating in that travel was made available to all members of the community. In June 1949, however, this was put onto a non-fare paying basis and confined to colliery employees only.

The coaches used on these trains were purchased from many pre-grouping companies and Ashington became noted for its range of vintage stock. Amongst those used were N.E.R. clerestory roof coaches dating from the turn of the century along with miscellaneous curved top stock from the Furness Railway, North Stafford, Great Western, London and North Western, and the Great Northern including an old directors' saloon of the latter.

Another really remarkable point about the passenger traffic was the density of the service. Trains ran almost continually between Hirst – Linton – Ellington although in recent times there was a gap in services between 2.30 a.m. and 6.00 a.m.! This may be more easily understood if one appreciates the vastness of Ashington's activities: it was to all intents and purposes an almost self-supporting coal producing community.

The colliery systems were all to standard 4' 8½" gauge but in the early days some interesting narrow gauge lines had been in existence. In 1880 a 2' 0" line was built to carry miners between Pegswood and Ashington and operated by a Fowler 0-4-2ST named *Bothal*. Six years later another line was constructed for the conveyance of coal to the workmen's homes

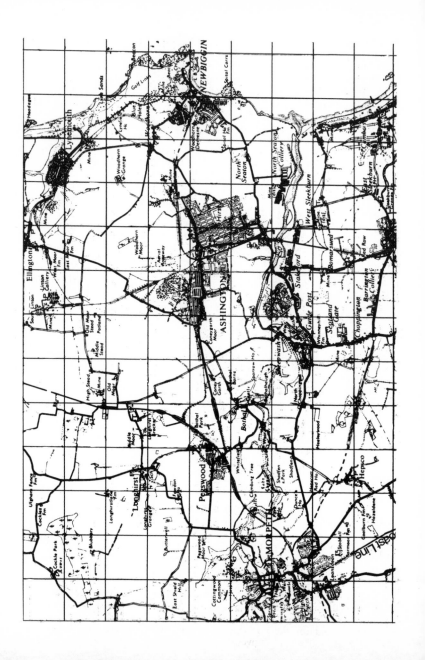

and during the process actually ran along Ashington's main street. It was operated by a Black Hawthorn 0-4-2ST. In 1907 extensions within the town necessitated the removal of this line to a new route and after the re-opening an Andrew Barclay 0-4-2T took over. The line was finally closed in 1936 when road transport undertook local coal deliveries.

The locomotive tradition at Ashington has been as rich as its coalfields and the system has provided immense interest for almost 100 years. In common with many other collieries the 0-6-0 tank type of both side and saddle construction has been favoured. Over the years a wonderful variety of designs was to be found, more than half of which were purchased second-hand. Between 1880 and 1958 over 70 steam locomotives worked on the system, of which 28 were purchased new, 36 second-hand, and 10 acquired on loan. This total involved as many as 40 different types from a wide range of builders.

It is of interest to note some of the second-hand engines purchased from pre-grouping companies:

Original Building date	Year Purchased	Last Example Withdrawn	Type	Quantity	Original Company(ies)
1872	1892	1913	0-6-0ST	1	North Eastern
1884	1923	1939	0-6-0T	4	Hull & Barnsley
1900	1929	1943	0-6-0ST	1	Alexandra Dock Railway, Great Western
1917	1929	1951	0-6-0T	1	Brecon & Merthyr, Great Western
1885	1931	1938	0-6-0T	1	North Eastern, London & North Eastern J74
1891	1932	1954	0-6-0T	1	London, Brighton & South Coast, Southern Railway E1
1894	1935	1962	0-6-0PT	2	Barry Railway, Great Western
1919	1937	1956	0-6-2T	2	Glasgow & South Western. London, Midland & Scottish
1886	1938	1953	0-6-0T	2	Great Eastern, London & North Eastern Railway J66

The Ashington Coal Company's locomotives had a green livery but during the second world war they were painted in black with white frames. The white frames were necessary to enable the locomotives to be seen during the blackouts when all lamps on the system were hooded. The later National Coal Board livery was blue.

Two principal designs of locomotives have been favoured since the 1940s: these were the Hunslet Austerity type 0-6-0STs and a larger outside cylinder 0-6-0ST from Robert Stephenson and Hawthorn. Some of the former were converted at Ashington to use Giesl ejectors. The two types are illustrated by plate nos. 104, 109 respectively.

Another interesting type delivered in 1954 was comprised of two handsome side tank locomotives with outside cylinders, also by Robert Stephenson and Hawthorn. These were purchased for operating the passenger services and one, No. 40, may be saved for preservation. The type is illustrated on plate no. 105.

Further locomotive interest was added to the system in 1959 when new area workshops were built at Ashington for the Northumberland Division of the N.C.B. These replaced the original workshops that had been situated at Linton. The works overhauled locomotives from many other collieries in the district along with waggons and general colliery equipment. (Plate nos. 104, 105.)

The last new steam locomotive to be purchased was No. 43 in 1956 which was built as an oil burner but was converted to coal fuel in 1959.

The fascination of the system began to diminish, however, after 1959 when 3 new diesel locomotives arrived and by 1966 5 were in operation. By the late 1960s Ashington's locomotive stock had become rather standardised and was principally made up of the following:

7 Austerity Type 0–6–0STs Some of which were fitted with Giesl ejectors and all with Stone steam generators for electric light.

The diversity of the Austerity Class is well illustrated by the fact that 4 different builders had been responsible for the 7 engines, namely Robert Stephenson & Hawthorn, Vulcan Foundry, Hunslet, and Andrew Barclay. The numbers were as follows: 27, 33, 44, 48, 50, 54, 55.

5 18″ Robert Stephenson & Hawthorn 0–6–0STs all of which had Stone steam generators and were numbered: 37, 38, 41, 42, 43.

2 Robert Stephenson & Hawthorn Outside-cylinder 0–6–0Ts Nos. 39 and 40. For passenger duties and also fitted with Stone steam generators.

2 Robert Stephenson & Hawthorn Inside-cylinder 0–6–0Ts Nos. 29 and 31. These were of an unusual design and possessed rather large driving wheels, and had cut-away side tanks to give accessibility to the inside motion.

In 1969 a preservation deal was made for purchase of No. 5 by the North Norfolk Preservation Group. This engine was a Peckett 0–6–0ST built in 1939 to that company's 0X1 Class.

It was noted earlier that main line engines frequently worked onto the system and some of the better known classes to appear were ex-N.E. J21, J25 and J27 0–6–0s and the Q5 and Q6 0–8–0s. During the twentieth century over 50 different types were recorded as having worked on to the system from either the N.E.R., L.N.E.R. or B.R. In the later years these included such classes as B1 4–6–0s, Stanier 8F 2–8–0s and even an A3 Pacific.

Notwithstanding this, the Ashington engines performed numerous duties and were kept fully employed, over half of them being scheduled to operate a continual 24-hour service. The control centre at Ashington directed operations over the entire system. Their duties included conveying the coals from the various collieries to the washing plants at Lynemouth or Ashington along with train loads of stone and shale which also went to the washeries to salvage the coal content. With these operations completed, the empties were returned to the various collieries as required. The locomotives were also used for internal goods traffic which included transferring of timber and various stores to the system's collieries whenever needed.

Further duties included working loaded and empty trains up to the main lines in addition to operating a large land sales depot. The sidings on the Ashington system had a vast storage capacity and coal of all grades was distributed for storage in readiness for future requirements.

Intermingled with the coal movements were the passenger trains, and as many as 20 daily return journeys were made on the Ashington – Linton – Ellington section. The company did not operate passenger services between Ashington and Woodhorn owing to the existence of the ex-N.E.R. line from Blyth to Newbiggin.

The Ashington passenger service was discontinued in 1966 in favour of bus transport and after lying idle the majority of the vintage coaching stock was broken up and by 1970 only the frame of a L.N.W.R. coach built at Wolverton in 1898 remained. This had been taken over by the platelayers' department. In 1968 the line from Newbiggin to Lynemouth along with the collieries at Linton was closed and the following year brought the-closure of the Coneygarth and Longhirst Drifts. The closures were largely the result of a reduction in availability of good seams. By 1970 the daily output had fallen to some 6,000 tons – a marked decline from the figure of 13,000 tons of the 1930s.

Also in 1969 came the arrival of more diesels in the form of 10 Paxman Hydraulic locomotives from British Railways, 9 for colliery operations and one to be cannibalised for spare parts. They had been built at Swindon in 1964/5 but had become redundant on British Railways at the time of their sale to the N.C.B.

Within a year of their being put into operation at Ashington the steam stock was reduced to two locomotives and one of the official reasons given for the dieselisation was compliance with the regional smoke abatement campaign.

In the early part of 1970 however 4 locomotives survived, two of which were withdrawn at the beginning of that year, Nos. 40 and 42. The former was set by for possible preservation by the same Group that acquired the Peckett, whilst the latter was cut up during March by Cole and Co. of Sheffield. The last two steam engines to operate the system are Nos. 41 and 43.

Although many changes have been made at Ashington it remains a thriving system in a somewhat uncertain industry. Today some coals are still exported from Blyth and the colliery also supplies a large quantity of small coals to the Cambois Power Plant. Despite the passing of much of Ashington's railway heritage it may be possible for some years yet to find the odd steam engine eking out its existence amid these ancient north-eastern coalfields.

A SELECTION OF PRESERVED COLLIERY LOCOMOTIVES

Locomotive	Type	Builder	Date Built	General Details	Place of Preservation
ELLESMERE	0–4–0WT	Hawthornes of Leith	1861	At work until 1957 in a Lancashire Colliery	Scottish Railway Preservation Society, Falkirk
No. 3	0–6–0ST	Fox Walker and Co.	1874	A vintage tank design at work until the 1960s at Mountain Ash Colliery, S. Wales	Destined for Bristol Museum
BELLEROPHON	0–6–0WT	Richard Evans	1874	A fascinating Well Tank locomotive which survived until the mid 1960s	Keighley and Worth Valley Railway
HAYDOCK	0–6–0T	Robert Stephenson and Co.	1879	A locomotive from the Haydock Collieries, Lancashire	Penrhyn Castle Museum
No. 28	0–6–2T	Taff Vale Railway	1897	A locomotive with an interesting history. Originally built for the T.V. Railway it passed into G.W.R. ownership at the grouping and was later sold to the Longmoor Military Railway where it acquired the name 'Gordon'. Its working career ended on the N.C.B.'s Durham area coalfield after which it was returned to S. Wales for preservation	South Wales Switchgear Co., Caerphilly
No. 39	0–6–0ST	Robert Stephenson and Hawthorn	1938	Ex Gedling Colliery on the Notts Coalfield	Foxfield Light Railway
No. 5	0–6–0ST	Peckett	1939	From the Ashington Colliery System, Northumberland	North Norfolk Railway Co. Sheringham

Some original colliery locomotives may be found under Preserved Locomotives on page 157

THE RAILWAYS OF
FRANCE AND GERMANY

The S.N.C.F. and the D.B.

Elsewhere in this volume various references have been made to the railways of France and Germany and it would be of interest very briefly to consider their histories.

Although Britain gave birth to railways as we know them today, the year 1827 saw the first line operative in France. Like the British, the French Railways were left to private enterprise but at all times during their history they were under much more government influence than their English counterparts.

It was largely due to this influence that very few main line companies ever appeared and those that were in operation were consequently of considerable size. Generally speaking each company served a different part of the country, thereby cutting out much of the competition and permitting a free interchange of ideas.

After the amalgamation of many small concerns the important companies were all in existence by 1857 and may be summarised as under.

Company	Formation Date	Principal Districts Covered
EST	1854	Paris, Reims, Belfort, Troyes, Nancy
NORD	1842	Paris, Amiens, Calais, Lille, Dunkerque
OUEST (Later ETAT)	1855	Paris, Versailles, Le Mans, Rouen, Brest, Cherbourg, Le Havre, Rennes
PARIS ORLEANS	1848	Paris, Orléans, Nantes, Bordeaux
MIDI	1852	Bordeaux, Irun, Toulouse, Narbonne
P.L.M.	1850	Paris, Nevers, Clermont-Ferrand, Lyon, Nice, Marseille, Nîmes

In addition to the above was one small state-owned line in the west of France which absorbed the Ouest in 1908 after the latter had got into financial difficulties. This action created the Etat as is shown in the above table. The system remained state controlled.

One other part of the French system consisted of the Alsace and Lorraine Railways which had been taken over by Germany in the Franco-Prussian war of the 1870s. After World War I these were returned to France and became a second state railway known as the Alsace and Lorraine.

It is surprising that, notwithstanding the insignificance of outside competition and the almost complete lack of inter-company rivalry, only three of the private concerns were in a satisfactory financial condition in the early part of the present century. They were the P.L.M., Nord and the Est.

The ravages of the First World War inevitably led to large claims upon the government for compensation which in turn led to closer state control and more unification between the companies. This involved such matters as standardisation of financial administrations and some uniformity of operation and equipment.

In 1934 the Paris–Orléans and Midi combined to form the Paris–Orléans–Midi (P.O.M.) and four years later on 1 January 1938 as a further step in the Government's control, complete nationalisation took place and thus was formed the S.N.C.F. – Société Nationale des Chemins de Fers Français (French National Railways). In this arrangement the government held 51% of the capital. Under the S.N.C.F. a regionalisation policy was adopted which was based on the territories of the old companies and was set out as follows.

No.	Region	Old Company
1	EST (Eastern)	Est. Alsace & Lorraine
2	NORD (Northern)	Nord
3	OUEST (Western)	Etat
4	SUD OUEST (South Western)	Paris–Orléans–Midi
5	SUD EST (South Eastern)	Paris–Lyon–Méditerranée
6	MEDITERRANEE (Mediterranean)	Coastal Regions of the Midi and P.L.M.

This system remains in operation today.

The vast damage caused to the French Railways during World War II accelerated their modernisation scheme as many aspects of their system had to be rebuilt. This caused the electrification of most principal routes and the dieselisation of secondary ones. The culmination of this is a situation in which they expect to have eliminated steam power completely by the end of 1971. France still retains a few small privately owned railways of both narrow and standard gauge.

Prior to the First World War the German Railways were largely the property of the individual states such as Prussia, Bavaria, Saxony and Baden.

After this war the German government was obliged as a part of the Treaty of Versailles to make reparations to France and Belgium in the form of 5,000 locomotives and 150,000 waggons. General indemnities had to be paid to the allied countries and it was felt that the German railway system could constitute a principal source.

Understandably the war had seriously damaged Germany's railways and in order for the demand to be met the allies enforced nationalisation.

It is a surprising fact that 75% of the reparations were paid in this way.

From 1 April 1920 the railways were unified as one system for the whole of the Republic under the direction of a national Ministry of Transport and known as the Reichsbahn (State Railway). At this juncture it is interesting to note the effect that this had on locomotive policy for this was the direct reason for the high degree of standardisation of German locomotive types today.

Only 19 years were to pass before the Second World War broke out in 1939 which led to the defeat of Germany and the dividing of the country into two parts. The West German Railways became the Deutsche Bundesbahn (German Federal Railway) (D.B.) and the East German the Deutsche Reichsbahn (German State Railway) (D.R.).

Today the D.B. operates under 16 Direktions (Regions) which are as follows:

Augsburg   Essen   Frankfurt   Hamburg   Hannover   Karlsruhe
Kassel   Köln   Mainz   Munich   Munster   Nürnberg   Regens-
burg   Saarbrücken   Stuttgart   Wuppertal

The D.B. today has a modern and highly efficient railway system and the country possesses a dense network. Much electrification and dieselisation have taken place and plans are scheduled for more extensive electrification. Nevertheless the D.B. still owns some 1,000 steam locomotives which are maintained in an excellent mechanical condition and still perform magnificent tasks. A startling fact about the D.B. is that at the beginning of 1970 a 12% increase in steam working occurred when an act of government passed much heavy traffic from road haulage to rail. This act necessitated the renovation of 100 steam locomotives which had been scheduled for withdrawal.

The D.B. expect to eliminate steam power in 1975.